ADVANCED
FACILITATION
STRATEGIES

ADVANCED FACILITATION STRATEGIES

Tools & Techniques to Master Difficult Situations

INGRID BENS, M.ED.

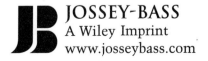
JOSSEY-BASS
A Wiley Imprint
www.josseybass.com

Published by Jossey-Bass
A Wiley Imprint
989 Market Street, San Francisco, CA 94103-1741   www.josseybass.com

Jossey-Bass books and products are available through most bookstores. To contact Jossey-Bass directly call our Customer Care Department within the U.S. at 800-956-7739, outside the U.S. at 317-572-3986, or fax 317-572-4002.

Jossey-Bass also publishes its books in a variety of electronic formats. Some content that appears in print may not be available in electronic books.

Library of Congress Cataloging-in-Publication Data

Bens, Ingrid.
    Advanced facilitation strategies : tools & techniques to master difficult situations / Ingrid Bens.
        p. cm.
    Includes bibliographical references.
    ISBN-13: 978-0-7879-7730-6 (alk. paper)
    ISBN-10: 0-7879-7730-6 (alk. paper)
    1. Teams in the workplace. 2. Group facilitation. I. Title.
HD66.B4448 2005
658.4'022—dc22   2005010922

Printed in the United States of America
FIRST EDITION
PB Printing   10 9 8 7 6 5 4 3 2 1

Contents

4 – Consulting Strategies for Facilitators

5 – Essential Processes for Facilitators   193

Introduction

OVER THE LAST FEW DECADES, THERE HAS BEEN a rapid growth in awareness about the importance of facilitation. While it was once an obscure skill, relevant mainly to consultants and human resources professionals, *facilitator* is now a common title being added to a growing number of job descriptions.

A great deal of the growth in facilitation is due to the use of teams in the workplace, especially those formed to improve productivity. While facilitation was once seen as a nice-to-have soft skill, team leaders have come to recognize that it is in fact a core competency, essential for achieving results in groups.

In addition, a growing variety of staff roles are transitioning out of direct service provision and functioning more as internal consultants. This is common in technology departments, human resources functions and financial services to mention but a few. In each of these cases, professionals find themselves in need of facilitation skills so that they can support the work of their clients.

Another major trend driving the growth of facilitation is the ongoing flattening of organizational structures. When employees work inside a single department they typically attend a small number of routine internal meetings. Today, employees often work on a variety of committees and project teams simultaneously, each of which hold meetings to coordinate member efforts.

The ever-expanding sphere of facilitation is indicative of the transformation in how work gets done in today's organizations: less through controlling and directing, more through coordinating and collaborating.

Meetings and more meetings seems to be the inescapable reality of working in today's interconnected workplace. Meetings to share information, plan strategy, coordinate work efforts, solve problems and develop working relationships.

To be effective in this highly interactive and demanding environment, virtually everyone needs to become highly skilled, very quickly. While some people may be able to get by with only rudimentary facilitation skills, most need to operate at a more advanced level. This is due to the fact that even the simplest meeting can unexpectedly become complex.

What Is Advanced Facilitation?

The differences between the beginner and advanced level are described in considerable detail in Chapter One of this book. In summary, advanced facilitators possess:

- a personal philosophy of facilitation
- a high degree of self-awareness and personal comfort based on practice and feedback
- knowledge about the stages of the facilitation process
- familiarity with a wide range of process tools
- the ability to create effective process designs and adapt them as circumstances change
- the ability to structure and lead complex decision-making processes
- the ability to manage dysfunctional behaviors and make effective interventions

The Goal of This Book

This resource has been created to help facilitators attain the advanced skills they need in order to deal with complex situations. It builds on the materials contained in *Facilitating With Ease! (*Jossey-Bass, 2nd edition, 2005) and provides tools and techniques that take facilitators to the next level of mastery.

While *Facilitating With Ease!* is a comprehensive, introductory textbook that aims to outline core skills, *Advanced Facilitation Strategies* is a practical field guide that offers strategies to deal with complex dilemmas. While references are made throughout this book to the experts who have given facilitation its theoretical underpinnings, the strategies described in this resource represent practical techniques found to work in everyday situations. These strategies are based on experience gained in hundreds of facilitated activities in organizations of all sizes and in all sectors.

The Audience for This Book

This resource has been created for any facilitator in need of strategies to deal effectively with complex challenges. This includes:

- project leaders who need to overcome apathy and create buy-in at the start of a new project
- supervisors who find that their staff meetings lack synergy
- managers frustrated that consensus is difficult to achieve
- community leaders who struggle to get group members to assume responsibility
- teachers coping with inattentive or unruly participants
- external consultants who encounter resistance because they're seen as outsiders
- internal consultants who feel they lack the power to facilitate upper management groups
- Human Resource professionals who manage complex systems change

This book is also a useful resource for anyone who hires facilitators or oversees the work of consultants, since it provides useful benchmarks for measuring third party performance.

The Assumptions Guiding This Book

This book is based on the following assumptions about you. It assumes that:

- you're aware of the foundational concepts of facilitation and you don't need to revisit basic meeting design principles and core tools
- you have had first-hand experience designing and leading meetings
- you have access to introductory textbooks about facilitation such as *Facilitating With Ease!* where you can access the core tools and techniques mentioned throughout this book
- you want to become better at diagnosing facilitation assignments and creating effective designs
- you want to broaden your repertoire of tools so you'll be able to make impromptu design changes whenever they're needed
- you want to become more resilient and confident when dealing with difficult situations and dysfunctional people

Content Overview

Advanced Facilitation Strategies consists of five chapters, plus a collection of surveys and evaluation instruments to be found on the accompanying CD-ROM.

Chapter One – Advanced Strategies Overview – In this chapter, each facilitator is encouraged to develop a personal philosophy of facilitation and identify the specific skills that they need in order to progress to the advanced level. Strategies are offered to deal with dilemmas in facilitation such as how to deal with the inherent powerlessness of the role, how to maintain neutrality in various situations and how to deal with group leaders. Chapter One also features an exploration of the connections between facilitation, consulting and the field of Organization Development.

At the end of the chapter there is an outline of the main practices that characterize the advanced level. Observation sheets and personal checklists are provided as handy references and guides.

Chapter Two – The Complexities of Decision Making – Chapter Two focuses on the important facilitator function of supporting groups in their quest to make effective decisions. The key strategy of shifting group focus is described along with specific examples of how this tactic can be deployed. Six common decision dilemmas are described in detail along with suggestions about how advanced facilitators resolve each one. Additional information is provided about core decision methods including ideas to overcome problems with consensus.

Chapter Two features a number of charts that summarize the typical steps in decision making, the tools associated with decision making and evaluation instruments for assessing the decision-making ability of groups.

Chapter Three – Conflict Management Strategies – Chapter Three describes various sources of group conflict and the mistaken assumptions commonly made by novice facilitators. It then describes nine different categories of tools that facilitators can use to intervene in order to bring order to group struggles.

Since conflict management skills are vitally important to the advanced facilitator, this chapter graphically describes thirty meeting situations that facilitators encounter on a regular basis and offer detailed and graphic suggestions for dealing with each scenario.

Chapter Four – Consulting Strategies for Facilitators – This chapter introduces the steps in the facilitation process and advocates their use in managing complex assignments. Each of the five steps, assessment, design, contracting, implementation and follow-up, is described in terms of how that step unfolds, its purpose, the main activities and the potential challenges. Tools, templates and checklists are provided to help the facilitator navigate each stage. Valuable advice is also offered about dealing with specific dilemmas that can arise at various stages.

Chapter Five – Essential Processes for Facilitators – All advanced facilitators need to know the steps in the most pervasive process and be aware of how they unfold. Chapter Five features process maps that outline the steps in the 14 processes central to facilitation work. In addition to the maps, the main steps in each process are detailed as well as some mention of key tools associated with that step.

To further enhance the value of this book as a flexible tool kit, the accompanying disk has been loaded with over one hundred of the charts, graphs, checklists and summaries located within the book. This CD-ROM also contains a collection of surveys and evaluations that can be customized to suit specific situations. To support facilitators with complex design work, the disk also features ten sample agendas, complete with process notes.

The need for collaboration and skilled facilitation has never been greater than it is in today's complex workplace. I hope that this resource serves as a valuable toolkit to all practitioners striving to enhance their personal competence!

Ingrid Bens, M.Ed.
May 2005

Some Definitions

Facilitator:
One who contributes structure and process to interactions so groups are able to function effectively and make high-quality decisions. A helper and enabler whose goal is to support others as they achieve exceptional performance.

Consultant:
A person in a position to have influence over individuals, groups or organizations, but who has no direct power to make changes or implement programs.

Manager:
A person who has direct power to make changes or implement programs.

Client:
The organization, group or individuals whose interests the facilitator/consultant serves.

Intervention:
Any action or set of actions taken to improve a situation. Can refer to action taken in the moment to redirect dysfunctional behavior or to a planned sequence of activities undertaken with the aim of initiating or introducing change.

Organization Development:
O.D. is a planned effort to increase organization effectiveness and health through planned interventions in the organizations processes using behavioral-science knowledge. O.D. interventions can be conducted on an organization-wide basis, focus on a single department or activity, apply at the small-group level or be used on an individual basis.

Organizational Development:
Not to be confused with O.D., organizational development is any effort to improve an organization such as traditional management consulting studies or externally driven change events. Unlike O.D., these efforts do not necessarily adhere to the same principles and practices as O.D.

Culture:
Basic assumptions and beliefs that are shared by members of an organization, that operate unconsciously, and that define an organization's view of itself and its environment.

Sponsor:
One who underwrites, legitimizes and champions a change effort or O.D. intervention.

Stakeholder:
One who has an interest in an intervention or its outcome. Stakeholders include customers, suppliers, distributors and employees.

System:
A series of interdependent components. Organizations that receive information from the environment are considered to be open systems. Systems also release outputs into the environment in the form of goods, services, information or people.

Sub-system:
Any part of a larger system such as a work unit, department or division. Sub-systems can be vertically integrated or they can be teams, processes or other activities that cut across an organization.

1
Advanced Strategies
Overview

WhEN WE FIRST SET OUT TO LEARN SOMETHING NEW, it's very helpful to have simple guidelines to follow: charts and graphs, checklists and straightforward tables of do's and don'ts. Whenever we begin to explore a new topic we want samples to copy and models to emulate: recipes that tell us exactly what to do.

But recipes and prescribed formulas have their limitations. Think of the cook who can only produce a meal by following a recipe. What if some of the essential ingredients are missing? What if other ingredients are available instead? What if more people turn up than expected?

While the novice cook knows how to follow recipes, the master chef knows how to work with whatever's available. He or she has an intimate knowledge of a wide range of ingredients and how they react to each other in different combinations and at various temperatures. The expert chef has what the amateur cook does not: a deep understanding of the principles of cooking and intimate knowledge about a wide range of ingredients and how to use them in different situations.

In facilitation, as in cooking, things don't always go as planned! Factors that were originally thought to be unrelated can unexpectedly emerge as central issues. The subject being discussed may suddenly reveal itself to be far more complex than previously thought. Group members may begin to exhibit counterproductive behaviors without apparent cause. The process that you designed so carefully can suddenly unravel!

> **Even the simplest facilitation can unexpectedly become complex!**

Since any discussion has the potential to become complex, it's essential that all facilitators move beyond the basics as soon as they possibly can. This means increasing your knowledge of the core principles of process leadership and knowing which strategies will work when the going gets tough.

This book aims to support you in your personal journey to the advanced level by offering you techniques and strategies to deal with a wide range of facilitation dilemmas. These include:

- the inherently powerless nature of facilitation
- the difficulty of gaining and keeping the role
- the challenge of working with upper management
- the overstressed and often resistant outlook of participants
- the difficulties inherent in making complex decisions
- the politics and hidden agendas present in many situations
- the dysfunctional behaviors that limit group effectiveness
- the challenge of providing structure to groups who may resist it

In today's fast-paced workplace, every conversation needs to be carefully designed and expertly executed in order to achieve maximum results. To do this you need to possess advanced strategies!

Your Personal Philosophy of Facilitation

It's logical to assume that the keys to becoming more skillful are to practice often, gather more tools and hone one's session design skills. While these activities are clearly important, the first step toward reaching the advanced level is actually the development of a personal philosophy of facilitation.

Having a clear set of principles and practices firmly in place will act like a foundation. It will ground you and make you more resilient in challenging situations. A clear personal philosophy will guide your interactions with others and provide you with a rationale when considering which elements to include in any design.

If you operate without a clear personal philosophy, you'll be lacking the organizing principle that will help you see patterns in your work. In this void you'll be randomly cobbling together tools and techniques in the hope that they create patterns of interaction that make sense. This need for clarity is further accentuated by the fact that there's still considerable confusion in the minds of many people about facilitation. This further accentuates why you must have a clear understanding of the purpose of your craft.

To help you develop a personal philosophy, consider adopting the following unassailable principles:

- Facilitation is grounded in a sincere respect for all group members regardless of their age, rank or cultural group.
- Facilitation is a transparent endeavor characterized by honesty and positive intent.
- Facilitators believe that everyone possesses innate wisdom that can be harnessed and channeled for the good of the whole.
- All facilitation activities aim to foster cooperation and commitment.
- Facilitators advocate empowerment and participation so that groups buy in and own the outcomes of their deliberations.
- Facilitators value the synergistic power of collective thought and strive to help groups arrive at collaborative decisions that represent a win for all parties.

Most important, facilitators never use the process role in order to seek personal power or control. The main goal of all facilitation activities is to enhance the effectiveness of others, whether that's the personal effectiveness of an individual who is being coached, the ability of a team to reach its goals, or the overall wellness of an organization and its culture.

The quest for a philosophy of facilitation is a personal journey that each of us needs to embark upon for ourselves. In addition to reading the works of leading thinkers in this field, you can begin by asking yourself some simple questions, such as:

"Why do I want to be a facilitator? What are my motives?"
"What do I bring to the people I facilitate?"
"What's unique about my work as a facilitator?"
"What elements must always be present in my work?"
"What actions or activities will I always exclude from my work?"
"What are the most important outcomes of my work?"

Once you've given this some thought, formulate a personal philosophy statement that you can share with others in order to clarify the principles that inform your work. This statement may evolve over time as your work matures and will always provide you with an anchor in times of doubt in the case of conflicting priorities.

My personal philosophy of facilitation:

The Three Levels of Competence

Increasing personal proficiency in any skill typically involves moving through a series of levels. Review the following description of facilitation skill levels and then complete the self-assessment that begins on page 7 to identify both your current competencies and the skills you most need to acquire.

Level I

New facilitators almost always start out leading the regularly scheduled meetings held within their own department or project team. These are meetings where they're familiar with the content under discussion and will be able to ask effective questions due to their knowledge of the issues being explored.

In these meetings the group leader is typically present, as are the facilitator's peers. The facilitator may be notified in advance to lead the meeting or, as is often the case, be pressed into action without much notice when the need for facilitation materializes.

The focus at Level I is:
- understanding the core principles, models and concepts of facilitation
- being able to manage a group discussion using core skills such as remaining neutral, asking questions, paraphrasing and summarizing
- having awareness of the key components of an effective meeting design
- knowing how to foster participation and encourage effective behaviors
- knowing when to use various decision-making tools
- making clear and accurate summaries and notes
- knowing various techniques for taking the pulse of the group in order to get things back on track

Level II

Once a facilitator has gained experience managing regular staff meetings, he or she may be asked to lead special purpose meetings for their peers or even for groups who are outside their work unit.

This transition can take place for a number of reasons. It can occur naturally simply because all groups have a periodic need for special purpose meetings such as problem-solving sessions, planning meetings, or team-building workshops.

This shift can also happen when a facilitator is sought out for assistance by those outside his or her immediate work group because they've gained a reputation for being effective. Regardless of the reason for the shift, leading more complex, special-purpose conversations requires an additional level of skill. This is especially true if the participants are unknown to the facilitator.

The focus at Level II is:

- knowing how to gather information, assess data and determine participant needs
- being aware of a wide repertoire of tools and techniques
- being able to design complex conversations
- being skilled at helping groups make difficult decisions and overcome decision blocks
- being able to manage a variety of complicated group dynamics without losing neutrality or personal composure

Level III

A facilitator is required to possess skills at the third and final level of mastery any time they're approached to design and lead processes that involve either a planned intervention to resolve a dispute, an initiative aimed at enhancing organizational effectiveness, or a planned change effort. Whether the assignment is internal or external to their usual work group, when a facilitator takes on a facilitation assignment that's part of one of these activities, they're functioning as an Organization Development consultant.

> **Organization Development is a planned effort to increase an organization's effectiveness and health through planned interventions in the organization's processes using behavioral-science knowledge. O.D. interventions can be conducted on an organization-wide basis, focus on a single department or activity, apply at the small-group level, or be used on an individual basis.**
>
> **(Beckhard, 1969)**

Note that the facilitator is now said to be acting as a consultant because they're acting to help or support a client through the application of their specialized knowledge in a situation where they lack managerial control. In the case of Organization Development consulting, that special knowledge is the application of process tools and techniques that are used to guide stakeholders through specific steps of the planned activity.

The focus at Level III is:

- possessing a personal philosophy of facilitation
- knowing about the core principles and practices of Organization Development
- being aware of the stages in the facilitation process
- being skilled at designing a wide range of data-gathering techniques
- knowing the key process models used to make interventions
- being able to design and facilitate complex, multi-stage interventions

Where Are You Now? – Self-Assessment

Begin your journey to facilitation mastery by reviewing the descriptions and competencies that follow. Identify both the skills that you currently possess and those areas in need of further development, then create your personal learning goals. The descriptions and competencies are arranged in three levels:

> Level I – consists of the core skills required to lead routine discussions and manage meetings effectively
>
> Level II – consists of the ability to design complex decision processes and manage difficult situations
>
> Level III – involves designing and leading activities that are part of a planned change effort

Level I - Basic Competencies Self-Assessment

New facilitators almost always start out leading the regularly scheduled meetings held within their own department or project team. These are meetings where they're familiar with the content under discussion and will be able to ask effective questions due to their knowledge of the issues being explored.

In these meetings the group leader is typically present, as are the facilitator's peers. The facilitator may be notified in advance to lead the meeting or, as is often the case, be pressed into action without much notice if the need for facilitation materializes.

1 = totally disagree	2 = disagree	3 = not sure	4 = agree	5 = totally agree

1. I understand the concepts, values and beliefs underpinning facilitation. ____

2. I'm aware of what to do at the start, middle and end of a facilitation ____

3. I'm skilled at active listening, paraphrasing, questioning and summarizing key points. ____

4. I'm able to manage time and maintain a good pace. ____

5. I know techniques for encouraging active participation and generating ideas. ____

6. I know how to create and then use group norms to encourage effective behaviors.   ____

7. I can make clear notes that accurately reflect what members have said.   ____

8. I'm familiar with the core process tools used to structure participative group discussions.   ____

9. I understand the difference between various decision-making tools and know when to use each one.   ____

10. I understand how to help a group achieve consensus and gain closure.   ____

11. I'm skilled at offering constructive feedback to groups and am comfortable accepting personal feedback.   ____

12. I know the key components of an effective meeting design and can create a detailed agenda.   ____

13. I know how to ask good probing questions that challenge assumptions in a nonthreatening way.   ____

14. I know when and how to conduct periodic process checks.   ____

15. I know how to use a variety of exit surveys to improve meeting effectiveness.   ____

Level I skills I currently possess:

Level I skills that I would like to develop further:

Level II – Intermediate Competencies Self-Assessment

Once a facilitator has gained experience managing regular staff meetings, they may be asked to lead special-purpose meetings for their peers or even for groups who are outside their work unit.

This transition can take place for a number of reasons. It can occur naturally simply because all groups have a periodic need for special-purpose meetings such as problem-solving sessions, planning meetings, or team-building workshops.

This shift can also happen when a facilitator is sought out for assistance by those outside their immediate work group if they've gained a reputation for being effective. Regardless of the reason for the shift, leading more complex, special-purpose conversations requires an additional level of skill. This is especially true if the participants are unknown to the facilitator.

1 = totally disagree	2 = disagree	3 = not sure	4 = agree	5 = totally agree

16. I know how to use surveys and conduct interviews to assess group needs and interests. ____

17. I can design meetings for a variety of purposes and can adjust my designs in mid-stream if necessary. ____

18. I know strategies to create a safe environment and gain buy-in from reluctant participants. ____

19. I can deal with resistance nondefensively, even when it's aimed at me personally. ____

20. I know the signs of 'group think' and can structure discussions to overcome it. ____

21. I'm skilled at asking complex probing questions that help members uncover underlying issues and information. ____

22. I can recognize the signs of group tension or conflict and do not hesitate to offer that insight to groups. ____

23. I'm able to appropriately and assertively intervene in order to redirect ineffective behavior. ____

24. I'm able to articulate both sides of an issue, then offer a process to reframe the conversation. ____

25. I'm able to hear and then consolidate ideas from a mass of information and create coherent summaries.   ____

26. I can recognize when decision processes are polarized and know how to restructure them so they're collaborative.   ____

27. I possess tools to help groups out of decision deadlocks.   ____

28. I understand the team development process and know how to implement a variety of team-building activities.   ____

29. I'm sensitive to interests, needs and concerns of individuals from different cultural backgrounds and from various levels and functions in the organization.   ____

30. I'm sufficiently versed in process responses that I never lose my neutrality even during difficult conversations.   ____

Level II skills I currently possess:

Level II skills that I would like to develop further:

Level III – Advanced Competencies Self-Assessment

A facilitator is required to possess skills at the third and final level of mastery any time they're approached to design and lead processes that involve either a planned intervention to resolve a dispute, an initiative aimed at enhancing organizational effectiveness or a planned change effort. Whether the assignment is internal or external to their usual work group, when a facilitator takes on such a facilitation assignment, they're functioning as an Organization Development consultant.

Note that the facilitator is now said to be acting as a consultant because they're acting to help or support a client through the application of their specialized knowledge in a situation where they lack managerial control. In the case of Organization Development consulting, that special knowledge is the application of process tools and techniques that are used to engage stakeholders in every step of the planned activity.

1 = totally disagree	2 = disagree	3 = not sure	4 = agree	5 = totally agree

31. I have a personal philosophy of facilitation that guides my work. _____

32. I'm aware of strategies for negotiating the power I need in order to be effective in any situation. _____

33. I understand the theories and primary methodologies of Organization Development. _____

34. I'm aware of the steps that make up the core processes that facilitators are asked to apply. _____

35. I'm aware of change management models and can use them to design and implement complex change activities. _____

36. I know how to design and facilitate various strategic and business planning discussions. _____

37. I know the steps in the main process tools that are part of process improvement efforts, such as process mapping. _____

38. I'm skilled at designing and implementing surveys. _____

39. I'm skilled at using survey feedback to involve clients to interpret their own data and identify actions. _____

40. I'm able to design and implement interpersonal and intergroup conflict interventions to settle contentious issues. _____

41. I'm aware of the steps in the coaching process and know how
     to use coaching to help individuals and teams.   ____

42. I'm able to deal comfortably with high-level management
     one-on-one and in group settings.   ____

43. I know how to contract for the use of my services as a neutral
     third party and operate as a process consultant.   ____

44. I'm able to design complex one- and two-day meetings and
     retreats to achieve specific outcomes   ____

Level III skills I currently possess:

Level III skills that I would like to develop further:

Combine the areas of further learning that you have identified in each of the three levels
to create a personal learning plan to guide you.

The skills and competencies that I plan to acquire or improve include:

_____

_____

_____

_____

_____

_____

The Power of Your Presence

In addition to possessing advanced tools and techniques, facilitators need to be conscious of the behaviors they exhibit and the image that they project. We have probably all known skilled facilitators whose performance was undermined because they unconsciously projected a negative attitude. To a great extent every facilitator's ability to be effective depends on how they're perceived.

When we stand in front of a group, all eyes are on us. As we work with them, people form an opinion about us. They decide if we're up to the task, if they can trust us, if they think we're sincere.

When a facilitator is an effective instrument for positive interaction, he or she projects a calm, confident demeanor. Their body posture is erect, without being stiff. They make appropriate hand and body motions that enhance or clarify what they're saying.

Skilled facilitators make ongoing eye contact with group members that's both comfortable and welcoming. By being candid and open they communicate that they are authentic in their interest in serving the group.

Accomplished process leaders show sensitivity by listening intently, noticing reactions and asking about feelings. They're never oblivious to concerns, but listen actively and don't hesitate to ask about feelings when it's helpful to do so.

If the atmosphere becomes strained, advanced facilitators show self-control and are able to refrain from becoming overly emotional. They're able to manage their own emotions, even in difficult situations. They never lose their temper, become embroiled in disputes, or show their displeasure.

Expert practitioners demonstrate their flexibility by constantly testing the process, offering options and adjusting activities. They pay attention to the proceedings and never get lost, forget key ideas, or allow themselves to become distracted.

Masterful facilitators are always unobtrusive, avoid the limelight and talk little, to ensure that member ideas dominate and so that the members feel a sense of ownership for the results of their deliberations.

Finally, advanced facilitators manage their personal energy so that the proceedings don't lose momentum. They strive to stay energetic and appear totally engaged throughout.

Your first step toward understanding what you project is to rate yourself on the instrument that follows. You could also ask a colleague to observe you in action and then offer specific feedback about how others see you.

Personal Projection Assessment

1. Personal demeanor

1_____2_____3_____4_____5

Nervous	Calm
Edgy	Confident
Unfocused	Organized

2. Body posture

1_____2_____3_____4_____5

Stiff or slouchy	Erect
Awkward	Coordinated
Tense	At ease

3. Hand and body gestures

1_____2_____3_____4_____5

Inappropriate	Appropriate
Distracting	Enhancing
Misleading	Clarifying

4. Eye contact

1_____2_____3_____4_____5

Rarely made	Continuous
Uncomfortable	Comfortable
Threatening	Welcoming

5. Authenticity

1_____2_____3_____4_____5

Closed	Open
Hidden motives	Candid
Insincere	Sincere

6. Sensitivity

1_____2_____3_____4_____5

Doesn't notice reactions	Notices reactions
Doesn't check feelings	Asks about feelings
Doesn't listen	Listens intently

7. Attending Behavior

1_____2_____3_____4_____5

Oblivious to concerns	Responds to concerns
Offers no feedback	Offers observations
Appears glum	Is upbeat and positive

8. Self-control

1_____2_____3_____4_____5

Overly emotional	Appropriate emotions
Loses temper	Remains neutral
Shows displeasure	Stays pleasant

9. Flexibility

1_____2_____3_____4_____5

Doesn't test	Tests the process
Alternatives not offered	Offers options
Forces preset direction	Adjusts constantly

10. Unobtrusiveness

1_____2_____3_____4_____5

Is the focal point	Is unobtrusive
Grandstands	Avoids the limelight
Talks a lot	Lets others talk

11. Focus

1_____2_____3_____4_____5

Gets lost	Pays attention
Loses key ideas	Manages input
Seems distracted	Totally engaged

12. Energy

1_____2_____3_____4_____5

Slows down	Maintains pace
Seems drained	Is energetic
Appears wan	Appears robust

What is O.D.?

Organization Development is a planned effort to increase organization effectiveness and health through planned interventions in the organization's processes using behavioral science knowledge. It was created in 1949 as a fusion of behavioral science and management theory. O.D. uses fundamental group processes to harness the wisdom and commitment of stakeholders to improve their own organizations. It's based on the belief that people are wise and will have more commitment to the plans or changes that they've designed for themselves.

The Key Principles and Practices

The essential principles of O.D. are listed below. You will note that these are completely coherent with the core beliefs of facilitation. These key principles are:

- People are healthy, self-motivated and capable.
- People will support what they create.
- Personal values must be examined.
- Everyone must respect the values of others.
- Interpersonal relations are critically important.
- Leadership style is important.
- Organization dynamics are important.

O.D. is totally holistic: it takes a systems view that asserts that all systems are connected and interrelated; that people are interrelated; that you can't change just one part of an organization. Organization Development is always viewed as an ongoing and continuous change effort whose overall aim is increased personal and organizational effectiveness.

The Core O.D. Activities

Whenever a facilitator leads discussions that are part of any of the following activities, he or she is in fact working as an O.D. practitioner:

- action research/diagnostic activities
- problem solving/process improvement
- strategy planning
- survey-feedback activities
- organizational restructuring, planning and goal setting
- techno-structural/work redesign activities
- managing change
- team building
- inter-group activities/negotiating

- leadership development
- coaching and counseling
- training linked to achieving change goals

In some cases an entire intervention may take place in a single meeting. An example of this might be a one-time team-building retreat. In other cases the facilitated meeting may be part of an ongoing series of discussions spread over several months. An example of this might be a process-improvement project.

Whether a meeting fits within a short or long time frame, it needs to be planned as part of a systemic change process that impacts the broader organization.

> **Aside from leading routine staff meetings all other facilitations are O.D. activities!**

To help you place your facilitation activities within this broader context of an O.D. intervention, this book provides the generic steps of O.D. processes in Chapter 5 and outlines the steps in the consulting process that are described in Chapter 4.

Learn More About O.D.

Since most facilitation activities take place within the context of an O.D. intervention, it's vitally important that all advanced practitioners become well read on this important topic. One of the most concise and easy to read handbooks on the subject is *Practicing Organization Development: A Guide for Consultants* by Rothwell, Sullivan and McLean. (1995, Jossey-Bass). The chapter references for Chapter 1 (p. 283) suggest additional titles that advanced facilitators may wish to read.

Working as a Consultant

Throughout this book, the facilitator is often referred to as the *consultant* while the participant is described as the *client*. This is in keeping with this idea of facilitation as a contracted role that has no intrinsic power or control over the situation other than the power that's been negotiated. Consider the definition of consulting provided by Peter Block in his seminal work *Flawless Consulting:*

> **"You are consulting anytime you are trying to change or improve a situation but have no direct control over the implementation. If you had control you'd be managing."**

In this context anytime you're asked to design, plan and lead a facilitated discussion that's part of a planned change effort and where you're an external third party, you're operating as a consultant.

Two Forms of Consulting

Before the field of O.D. was created, the dominant form of consulting was expert based. In this model the third party is brought in to assess a situation and offer their recommendations for action. O.D. created an alternative form of consulting in which the external third party does not offer advice, but provides the *processes* through which clients can create and implement their own plans.

Expert consulting	Process consultants
1. Preliminary diagnosis 2. Data gathering 3. Analysis by expert 4. Recommendations for action by consultant 5. Implementation	1. Preliminary diagnosis 2. Data gathering 3. Data feedback to clients 4. Data analysis by clients 5. Action planning by clients 6. Implementation by clients
The consultant offers content in the form of expert advice	The consultant offers processes and facilitates
The consultant is not neutral The consultant offers their expertise The consultant prescribes The consultant may manages implementation activities	The consultant is neutral The consultant brings process skills The consultant is nonprescriptive The consultant supports the client's efforts

Thinking of yourself as a consultant and managing your facilitation assignments using the steps of the consulting process that are outlined in Chapter 4 will not only help you manage your work, but will also generate a greater sense of professionalism. This is especially important if you are working as an internal facilitator.

The Connection to Facilitation

Since O.D. consulting is the application of process while remaining neutral on the content, it's easy to see that all facilitated discussions that aim to solve a problem, resolve a conflict, plan a strategy, or create change are essentially Organization Development activities. It is further also true that all O.D. practitioners are expert facilitators.

> **Most facilitation assignments are O.D. activities.**

Expanding Your Power Base

Those who are new to facilitation often operate under the mistaken assumption that being neutral about the content under discussion also means being neutral about the process. The result of this thinking is that many neophytes project such a sense of powerlessness that they end up as little more than scribes.

This power dilemma is most acutely felt by internal facilitators. While external process leaders are assumed to be credible and automatically given more authority, internal facilitators tend to have much less clout. To complicate matters further, internal facilitators often lead meetings attended by their peers and the managers to whom they report. These factors combine to inhibit internal facilitators from acting authoritatively.

Whether you're an internal or external facilitator, it's important that you're aware that facilitation is not a powerless role! While it's true that facilitators are impartial about the outcome of discussions, it's a mistake to extend this notion of neutrality to the process elements. The result of this mistaken thinking is that inexperienced facilitators often stand by mutely while participants ignore their agenda and interact dysfunctionally.

In contrast, experienced facilitators are much more assertive because they understand that neutrality refers only to the content elements. In addition to this they also know that:

> **The amount of power a facilitator has in any situation = the amount of power that they negotiate!**

This suggests two strategies:

1. Facilitators should always manage the process elements assertively, plus
2. Facilitators should always seek the additional powers they will need in order to work effectively.

To illustrate this principle, here's an example of a power negotiation between an internal facilitator and a group of senior executives:

> From your past experience with this specific group of upper managers, you know that they tend to grandstand, interrupt each other and ignore the process steps that they agreed to follow. In the past you've felt powerless to make interventions because you're in a relatively junior position and are concerned about offending senior leaders. Since you don't want to preside over a disastrous meeting, you start the session by engaging the group in a conversation about your role, saying something like:
>
> *I want this to be a productive and worthwhile meeting for you. In order for me to do my job well today, I need to clarify some things with you.*
>
> *If I sense that people aren't hearing each other's points, for example, I want to make sure it's okay for me to stop the conversation and get the parties to repeat each other's key ideas to make sure all ideas are heard.*
>
> *I also want to make sure that it's okay for me to stop any debates that get heated and ask people to restate their points in language that's more neutral.*
>
> *Finally, I want to ensure that it's seen as my role to point out when time limits are being ignored so we can get back on track.*
>
> *Are there any other situations that could come up at today's meetings and what is it okay for me to say or do in each situation?*
>
> As group members respond to your questions, they'll be basically ratifying your power to control the process. Make notes on a sheet of flip chart paper, taking special care to use any specific wording suggested by the members. Then post the list of your new powers in clear sight.

You may have recognized that this is a form of norming, known as a normative contract. In this example the normative contract is aimed at increasing personal leverage. Once you've completed these negotiations, the stage will be set for you to manage as assertively as necessary. Rather than being offended by your interventions, participants will feel that you're doing their bidding.

Why Negotiate Power You Already Possess?

It's important to note that you don't actually need the permission of participants to assertively manage things like behavior, since facilitators already have the right to manage the process elements. But we all know that theoretical power isn't necessarily power you can wield. The negotiation process is simply used in these cases to gain buy-in for your ability to exercise your role to its fullest extent.

In addition to affirming your power to assertively manage the process elements during discussions, facilitators can also negotiate other conditions surrounding their work. These negotiations will not only reduce confusion group members may have about your role, but will also allow you to have a say in the design of any interventions that you may need to make.

Some of the normative contracts that a facilitator might seek include:
- that key decision makers will be present
- that you will be granted full access to staff in order to gather background information from participants
- that group members will respect your process design and agree to adhere to it throughout the proceedings
- that the important elements of organizational support are in place before an activity proceeds
- that you will be given a role in managing the follow-up process

The notion of negotiating in order to gain additional power is described in more detail starting in Chapter 4 in the section on contracting for your services. It is also illustrated on page 98 in Chapter 3.

To help you identify opportunities to negotiate more power, identify the scenarios and situations in which you feel powerless as a facilitator. Next, identify the specific powers that you need in each of these situations:

When do I feel powerless?   What powers do I need in these situations?

Gaining the Authority to Facilitate

New facilitators are often unsure about just how much authority they possess when they're acting as a facilitator. This is especially true for people working inside organizations who haven't officially been given the title of facilitator. These folks wonder whether they have the authority to lead a group discussion and too often hold back their process expertise out of fear that they'll appear to be challenging the power of the group's official leader.

This concern is based on the assumption that facilitation is like other jobs that depend on having some form of official designation. It's also rooted in the fact that facilitation is essentially a powerless role with no inherent authority.

Advanced practitioners aren't bothered by this power vacuum. They know that they can obtain the right to facilitate in any situation. While it certainly helps to have a manager's approval or be officially assigned to be the facilitator for a specific group, a formal job description isn't needed to step into the role. What is needed is the consent of the people being facilitated.

> **Never forget that facilitation is leadership by consent!**

This consent can be gained in two ways: through formal negotiations during the contracting phase of any facilitation assignment or by simply offering to act as facilitator and having the group members accept. Once a group has agreed to be facilitated, that agreement is a form of contract whether it's a verbal contract for a single meeting or a detailed letter of agreement to facilitate a lengthy project.

If lack of official approval remains a major stumbling block to getting your expertise used, make facilitation skills a priority in your personal learning plan and ask your manager for opportunities to practice. More organizations are also creating volunteer cadres of internal facilitators that you may be able to join.

In summary, remember that:

- facilitation doesn't come with any inherent power beyond what's negotiated with group members;
- any official power of the person facilitating is outside the facilitation role;
- the role of facilitator doesn't need to be an officially designated role and has nothing to do with rank; and
- in order to facilitate you need only gain the consent of the participants.

Losing the Facilitator Role

Since facilitation power is relatively easy to gain, it's important to be aware that there's a flip side to that coin: namely, that it's equally easy to fall out of the role!

> **Gaining the role is the easy part . . .**
> **. . . keeping it is much harder!**

A facilitator can lose the role for a whole host of reasons:

- The process being used is based on insufficient information, the wrong information, or assumptions that were never tested.
- The design was created without being tested with the participants to gain their buy-in.
- The skills and experience of the facilitator do not match the difficulty level of the conversation.
- The facilitator failed to engage the group in setting the needed norms for the situation.
- The facilitator failed to be appropriately assertive in managing the process.
- The facilitator engages in unintentional behaviors that resulted in a loss of neutrality.

Unintentionally Losing Neutrality

One of the most common ways that facilitators lose the role is by unintentionally losing their neutrality concerning the content. This can happen in a number of ways:

Changing members' words – recording ideas that don't reflect what people are actually saying. Putting in words that you like better without ratifying them with the members. Rewriting reports to more closely reflect your views or the views of management.

Taking sides – saying things like *good idea* or *good point* when someone makes a comment you like without realizing that another member who has an opposing opinion now sees you as having taken sides.

Asking too many leading questions – or asking overly critical questions may undermine member confidence in their own opinions and steer them toward decisions for which they have no real commitment.

Unconscious selling – repeatedly making suggestions that may have been rejected by the group earlier. Offering suggestions in a way that doesn't feel neutral to members.

Not checking assumptions – moving forward without checking personal assumptions. Operating out of mistaken beliefs or with incomplete information. Operating out of one's own prejudices.

Answering content questions – instead of redirecting these questions to other group members or making a process response. Voicing opinions and joining into decision-making discussions.

Favoring one person or party over another – giving one person or party more time to present their ideas. Making eye contact with some people and not with others. Unintentionally encouraging one person or party more than another.

Raise your personal awareness of this important issue by reflecting on your past experience:

Have you ever lost the facilitator role in the middle of a meeting?

Which of the factors mentioned earlier contributed to your losing the role?

Maintaining and Regaining the Role

Since process leadership can easily be lost, it's important to have strategies to regain followership whenever it happens. The first step, of course, is to attune yourself to the signs that this has happened. Pay attention to body language signals that announce people are annoyed, frustrated, or have simply tuned out.

Since people are unlikely to speak up and announce that they've lost faith in either you or the proceedings, take a proactive approach by making periodic process checks. This involves stopping the action from time to time to ask:

Is this working? Are we on track? Are we making progress?
Is the tool we're using effective or should we try another technique?

Even when a facilitator asks for feedback, participants may be reluctant to speak out. In these situations try posting a midpoint check that allows people to make written, anonymous responses. When you invite participants to complete the survey, encourage them to be candid and assure them that their honest views are wanted. This activity is also illustrated on page 144 in Chapter 3.

---

1) To what extent are we making real progress at this meeting?

1_____2_____3_____4_____5
None   Some   Lots

2) Is the approach we're taking effective or do we need to try another technique?

1_____2_____3_____4_____5
It's not   It needs adjustment   It's working:
working   keep going

3) Is everyone being heard?

1_____2_____3_____4_____5
You've lost me!   We could do better   Everyone's
                                                ideas count

Once the survey has been completed, review the results with the members and ask:

1) Why did each question receive the rating that it got?
2) What can be done during the rest of the meeting to improve the ratings for each item?

Implement all of the ideas that are feasible and likely to help improve session effectiveness.

Midpoint checks are an important tool to add to your tool kit and an indispensable strategy for testing the quality of your work while there's still time to resolve problems. It should be a part of your design for all lengthy meetings. A further illustration of this strategy in action can be found on page 150 in the section on conflict management strategies.

Inviting Personal Feedback

If you sense that meeting problems stem from your process leadership, you could include a question that invites personal feedback, such as the one below:

To what extent do you have confidence in my ability to facilitate this session?

1_____2_____3_____4_____5

You've lost me!   I have a few suggestions   You're doing great!

If you sense that people might be reluctant to respond to a survey question about your performance, absent yourself from the room while one of the group members leads a short discussion that centers on the two questions above.

If the notion of asking for personal feedback seems too risky, weigh those risks against the danger of carrying on with a facilitation that feels like it isn't working. Carrying on like nothing's wrong, when there is a problem, sends the message that you can't read the group or deal confidently with conflict.

Creating a safe vehicle for group members to surface and help deal with a sensitive feedback situation sends the message that you are confident, can hear constructive feedback, and are capable of managing a challenging situation. This isn't an easy thing to do, but it is the strategy an advanced facilitator would apply!

The Two Types of Interventions

When a discussion encounters difficulty, it's the facilitator's job to make an intervention. Too often novice facilitators hesitate to take action because they worry that they lack the power to intervene or that they'll offend someone in the group.

Experienced facilitators know that making interventions is totally within the boundaries of the facilitator's role, does not violate their neutrality, and must be made whenever an ineffective situation threatens group effectiveness. Some examples of situations that require intervening include:

- a group making a hasty decision without sufficient data
- a group that throws out its process
- when the solution being proposed lacks the creativity or innovation required by the situation
- when group members fail to explore a wide range of possibilities because an influential member is pressuring them to accept the solutions they favor
- whenever member behaviors become ineffective and hamper progress.

Advanced facilitators are also aware that intervention responses fall into two categories, and they know when to use each type:

Content interventions	Process interventions
Offering expertise	Providing feedback
Making suggestions	Offering critiquing tools
Giving advice	Redirecting behaviors
Telling members what to do	Asking probing questions

When to Make Content Interventions

By definition, facilitation is a neutral process role. However, facilitators are often working in areas where they're experts. When this is the case and when the group is in need of additional information or expert advice, a content intervention may indeed be appropriate.

Stepping out of the neutral role to participate in the content is tricky since it may shift power away from group members toward the facilitator so that he or she ends up controlling the outcome.

To guard against this possibility, content interventions need to be made cautiously and intentionally. Here are some guidelines that may be helpful:

- Identify your specific expertise early in the planning stages and agree on when and how that expertise will be shared.
- Describe personal areas of expertise to participants at the start of any meeting where you might play both roles.
- Design the agenda so that expertise-sharing sessions are clearly segregated from group discussions.
- If there's an unexpected need for your expertise in the middle of a discussion, clearly state the you're stepping out of the facilitator role to offer expert advice.
- Always be clear whether you're sharing expert opinion or non-negotiable input:

Expert opinion is:	Nonnegotiable input is:
Explaining a preference based on your expertise Open to change	Something that's legislated or is a design feature that's not negotiable
"Based on my experience, I would choose . . . "	*"Here are the things that can't be changed or omitted . . . "*

Deepening Your Process Responses

One of the greatest challenges reported by new facilitators is remaining neutral when a meeting starts to flounder. These situations can precipitate an unintentional slip out of the neutral role to critique responses and even prescribe solutions.

Since facilitation is a helping role, the impulse to rescue a struggling group is only natural. Couple this with the fact that facilitators should never stand by idly while a group makes a disastrous decision, and it's easy to understand how readily neutrality can be violated.

While there are instances, such as those described earlier, where it's appropriate to step out of the neutral role to intervene in content, advanced practitioners possess a broad range of process interventions that preserve their neutral role.

> **Aside from situations where content is intentionally shared, advanced facilitators always intervene on the process level.**

Examples of Process Interventions

Situation	Process Intervention
The group makes a hasty decision without adequate data	Engage members in identifying the data that's needed to make an effective decision, then use this as a checklist to test the quality of the available options.
Members are taking positions and arguing emotionally to convince others they're right	Engage members in identifying the pros and cons of each proposal.
A questionable course of action is identified	Facilitate a discussion to name the key criteria for judging the quality of a solution. Assign weights to each criteria. Create a decision grid and test the course of action against each individual criteria element.
Members are stuck in old patterns and can't think *out-of-the-box*	Help members describe the traits of an innovative solution. Then ask people to put on other *hats* to identify creative solutions.
Members can't generate ideas	Identify the key questions that need to be asked. Organize members to find stakeholders to interview or best practice organizations to research. Bring back input to spark idea generation.
A course of action goes untested in a group with a track record for poor follow-through	Engage the members in a troubleshooting discussion to identify all of the things that could go wrong or could block progress. Ask members to identify how they contribute to these blocks and barriers, then help members identify a strategy or make a commitment to respond to each block or barrier.

Members are failing to think critically about the situation.	Ask a series of probing questions that make people think more deeply about the current situation and/or the impact of various courses of actions.
Member behaviors deteriorate and adversely affect group effectiveness.	Offer feedback about what you are noticing, then engage members in setting new norms aimed at getting members to act appropriately.

Identify the types of situations where you often find yourself slipping out of the neutral role to make unintended content interventions. Then identify some of the process responses you will use in future occurrences:

Anticipated situations: ⟶ **Process responses:**

_____   _____

_____ ⟶ _____

_____   _____

_____ ⟶ _____

_____   _____

_____ ⟶ _____

_____   _____

_____ ⟶ _____

_____   _____

_____ ⟶ _____

Managing the Role of Leaders

In order for any facilitated activity to be effective, the leader and the facilitator need to be crystal clear about each other's respective roles and responsibilities. There are a number of dynamics that make it a challenge to balance the roles of the leader and facilitator:

- Facilitators are usually asked to work with groups at the request of the leader. As a result, leaders often mistakenly assume that they're the client and that the facilitator is there to do their bidding.
- Leaders often request facilitation assistance but actually have an outcome in mind that they want the facilitator to lead the group toward.
- Leaders may indicate that they're prepared to give over process control, only to step in and try to control the flow, especially if the conversation shifts in a direction they don't personally favor.
- Leaders may indicate a readiness to empower and share control that they aren't actually prepared to accept.

Facilitators need strategies to deal with these scenarios:

- Facilitators need to clarify that the client is always the entire group, department, or team, including the leader, but is not exclusively the leader. This should be done verbally and reinforced in writing in advance of any assignment. All group members should be made aware that they, not just the leader, are the client of the facilitator.
- The facilitator needs to ask the leader if they have a specific outcome in mind, how open they are to innovative solutions, or if there are specific solutions that need to be classified as unacceptable.
- The facilitator needs to clarify his or her role in advance of the meeting so that both the leader and the other participants are clear that it's the facilitator's role to design and manage all process elements.
- The facilitator needs to share the four-stage empowerment chart with the leader to identify the level at which each conversation will be taking place:

    Level I – the group being told an outcome

    Level II – members being asked for their input to a decision to be made elsewhere later

    Level III – members being asked to make recommendations that require further management approval, or

    Level IV – members totally empowered to make an independent decision and take action without further approvals.

The strategy of clarifying empowerment levels is illustrated in greater detail on page 53 in Chapter 2 where strategies to clarify empowerment are provided.

When The Boss Is in the Room

In an ideal world, relations between leaders and staff would be so safe, open, and honest that everyone could confidently speak their mind with managers present. The sad truth is that most groups feel very inhibited in the presence of leaders.

Sometimes this is due to a past history of reprisals over comments made at meetings. In other cases the unease stems from a simple lack of experience with collaboration and dialogue between organizational levels. Whether this inhibition is real or just a perception, facilitators need strategies to ensure that conversations aren't hampered by the presence of leaders.

First, let's look at the pros and cons of having leaders present during facilitated conversations:

Pros	Cons
• their presence demonstrates their openness and commitment to collaboration	• the leader's presence may keep people from raising issues or identifying problems
• leaders have wisdom and expertise to add	• their presence may inhibit discussion and creativity
• they see the big picture	• the leader may dominate
• they can help the group access resources and remove barriers	• they may hinder member ownership

Asking leaders not to attend meetings is not only impractical, but also denies the group one of its most valuable resources. The key is to talk to leaders in advance about the potential downside of their participation to increase their awareness and enroll their support.

Here are some strategies to consider:

- Ask the leader to start meetings where staff input is being sought by making a statement that sets a positive and open tone. He or she could ask for lively debate and a free exchange of creative ideas.

- The leader could be invited to suggest some *safety norms* for the session such as:

    What's said in the room, stays in the room.
    Naming issues or problems in order to solve them is constructive.
    There will be no retaliation for any comments made in a problem-solving spirit.

- Reduce leader domination by coaching them to refrain from putting their ideas or solutions on the table too early or too often so they don't hinder input.

- Ask leaders to clearly announce when they're sharing expertise, offering information, or announcing a nonnegotiable item. Help them to see this as different from offering an idea or suggestion.

- Coach leaders to present their ideas as questions instead of statements, so as to encourage conversations rather than end them.

- Encourage the leader to switch from strictly playing the content role to taking up more facilitative functions like paraphrasing the comments of others, asking clarifying questions, posing probing questions, and asking quiet people for their input.

- The facilitation design should include a variety of discussion techniques that provide private avenues for sharing ideas. These include techniques like dyads, small groups, written brainstorming, multivoting and wandering flip charts.

- The meeting design could be divided into sections so that the leader can share valuable information, then leave during sensitive problem solving discussion. He or she can then return to hear recommendations for action and to offer their support.

- Finally, the leader should be encouraged to refrain from taking responsibility for action plans that are more suitably left to staff. Encourage the leader to play the role of champion to staff initiatives, which involves coaching, obtaining resources and removing barriers.

Above all, managing the participation of leaders shouldn't be left until the middle of the session when negative impacts of their presence have already had an effect on proceedings.

Enhancing Your Questioning Skills

Since facilitation is essentially a questioning function, it's not an exaggeration to say that a facilitator is only as good as the questions they ask! Asking a weak question may send a group in the wrong direction. Failing to ask the right probing questions may result in the group not exploring issues deeply enough. For this reason advanced facilitators must be extremely skilled at asking the right question at the right time.

Before launching into any line of questioning, always asks yourself:

> - *What do I want to ask?*
> - *Why do I want to ask this?*
> - *How might people respond?*

Regardless of the question type (open or closed) or the setting, here are some question development guidelines to consider:

- Always customize the questions to fit the context.
- Ask questions that people are capable of answering.
- Use language that's clear and unambiguous.
- Create safety before asking difficult questions.
- Stay open and avoid questions that lead people to specific conclusions.
- Ask follow-on questions that fit with the flow of the conversation.

Questions fall into a number of categories depending on what they're intended to do. In addition to the examples offered here, you will find dozens of examples of questions scattered throughout this book. Here are a few of the main categories of questions in common use:

Questions that set the context	*What's our goal at this meeting?* *What are your expected outcomes?*
Questions that invite development	*Can you say more?* *What else is connected to this?*
Questions that probe	*How did this start?* *Who's involved?* *What's the history of this?*
Questions that clarify	*Are you saying . . . ?* *Am I understanding that . . . ?*

Questions that diverge	*What would be the opposite of that?*
	What would the competition do?
Questions that reframe	*Can you say that in another way?*
Questions that link	*What else fits here?*
	What comes to mind that is similar?
	When did this happen before?
Questions that invite challenge	*Who sees it a different way?*
	What would our competitors say?
Questions that test	*What are the pros and cons of this?*
	What are the main blocks and barriers?
Questions that summarize	*What are the key ideas we can all live with?*
	What can we say to bring closure?
Questions that build buy-in	*What's in it for you?*
	What do you stand to gain?
Questions that overcome resistance	*What concerns you about this topic?*
	What conditions or assurances will overcome those concerns?

This large and complex topic deserves far more attention than can be provided given the scope of this book. For a resource devoted entirely to questioning take a look at *Questions That Work* by Dorothy Strachen (ST Press, 2001) for a comprehensive overview of this essential art. There is also an excellent overview of questioning in *The Secrets of Facilitation* by Michael Wilkinson (Jossey-Bass, 2004).

Asking Complex, High-Quality Questions

While novice facilitators are often overreliant on asking *why* or presenting simple questions, advanced facilitators tend to ask complex, high-quality questions that help the participants form a visual image of their response.

Here's an example of these two types of questions:

Low-quality, simple questions	High-quality, complex questions
What factors do we need to consider when ordering this year's camp supplies?	If we were going to provide every staff and member with exactly the right equipment to run exciting programs this year, what would each of them need?
What are the steps in the order-scheduling process?	Think about all of the steps that it takes to get an order to our customers. What's the first step in that journey?
What are the factors that contributed to the problems at this year's festival?	Think back to this year's festival and describe some of the glitches and frustrations that you experienced.
What would improve this plant?	Imagine that this plant is totally perfect! All the supplies and equipment are in place! All the systems are working! Describe what you see.

The Traits of Complex, High-Quality Questions

While there's nothing inherently wrong with simple straightforward questions like the ones in the left-hand column above, the questions in the right-hand column are more likely to evoke thoughtful response. The reasons for this are related to the structure of these comments:

- High-quality questions start with prompts like *Imagine that . . . Think back to . . .* or *What if . . .* that encourage participants to develop a clear picture of the scenario under discussion.
- High-quality questions are more personal and put the participant into the picture by using words like *you.*
- High-quality questions are less vague because they offer more details about the situation that's being explored.

Advanced facilitators also incorporate comments from group members to create a connected line of questioning. This makes the questioning sequence more organized and links it to the participants.

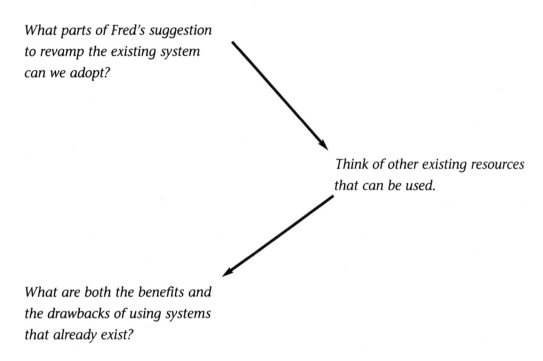

What parts of Fred's suggestion to revamp the existing system can we adopt?

Think of other existing resources that can be used.

What are both the benefits and the drawbacks of using systems that already exist?

As you move to a more advanced level of personal competence, you become more conscious of your questioning patterns:

- Are you asking complex, high-quality questions that paint a picture and engage participants?
- Are your questions sufficiently detailed to avoid confusion about what you're asking?
- Do you build on people's comments to create a connected line of questioning?
- Are you conscious of the purpose of each question: are you asking to invite, probe, clarify, reframe, diverge, test, challenge, or link?

Advanced Facilitation in Action

An important part of advancing to a higher skill level is incorporating specific techniques and behaviors into your work in front of groups. Since facilitation is such a highly personalized activity, it's not possible to dictate how or when to incorporate these various techniques into your personal practice.

Instead, think of the following as descriptions of some of the things that advanced facilitators say and do that distinguish them from beginners.

1. Advanced facilitators always clarify the purpose, process, and expected outcomes at the start of all discussions to ensure that there's a clear, shared focus.
2. They use norming in a very targeted way to set the climate, create safety, negotiate additional power, or enroll members to manage their own behavior.
3. Experienced facilitators confidently test their assumptions and check for buy-in from participants.
4. They paraphrase continuously to check for clarity and ensure that people feel heard.
5. Advanced facilitators ask complex, high-quality questions rather than relying on simple questions like *Why?* or *What else?*
6. Instead of keeping the process silent and hidden from participants, master facilitators verbalize it continuously so that participants know what they're doing and why.
7. Instead of recording the ideas of individuals, skilled facilitators *ping-pong* comments around the group to create synergistic, multidirectional conversations.
8. Instead of wondering how things are going, master facilitators make frequent checks to test the purpose, the people, the process, and the pace.
9. Instead of tolerating dysfunctional behavior, advanced facilitators make appropriate interventions calmly and without hesitation.
10. They're excellent at making clear notes and offering accurate summaries at the appropriate time in discussions.
11. Expert facilitators know how to help groups achieve closure in decision-making discussions, as well as help groups test the quality of their decisions.
12. They ensure that detailed action plans are in place and that blocks to implementation have been considered.

To further assist you in adding these elements to your repertoire, each practice is described in more detail on the pages that follow and are summarized on the observation sheet on page 39. This observation sheet can be used as a personal checklist or as a coaching tool.

Advanced Skills Observation Sheet

Behaviors   **Notes**

Clarifies the purpose and expected outcomes

Clearly explains the process

Is open to negotiating the purpose and process

Makes sure the appropriate norms are in place

States/checks assumptions

Tests for resistance and buy-in

Paraphrases continuously

Asks complex, high-quality questions

Continuously verbalizes the process

Ping-pongs conversation to create synergy

Periodically checks the process

Periodically reclarifies the purpose

Periodically asks how people are doing

Periodically asks about the pace

Is energetic and maintains a good pace

Assertively makes appropriate interventions

Makes clear notes

Offers accurate summaries

Helps the group achieve closure

Helps the group test the quality of outcomes

Helps create clear and doable action plans

Debriefing Your Experience

No one becomes a master facilitator without experiencing their share of disasters! Don't let those experiences deter you. The key is to glean valuable lessons from each one. After a particularly difficult facilitation, spend some time reflecting on what happened. Ask yourself:

☐ Did I do enough research about the client, their history, and culture? Did I really understand the group and its issues?

☐ Did I have a good sense of the personalities in the group – who might act out and their motives for doing so?

☐ Did I identify my assumptions about the group? Did I ever check them out, or did I hold on to them even when it became obvious that some of them were wrong?

☐ Did I prepare a detailed process outline for myself that included alternative approaches?

☐ Did I do a thorough job of clarifying the goal and the specific objectives of the meeting at the start, before jumping in?

☐ Did I explain my role and gain the authority and support I needed to run the meeting effectively?

☐ Did I review the norms with the group and ask targeted norming questions to head off difficulties that might arise?

☐ Did I get buy-in at the start of the meeting to make sure that people felt connected to the session?

☐ Did I do periodic process checks even when things seemed to be going well? Did I, for example, ask if we were making progress? Ask if the pace felt right or if the approach seemed to be working?

☐ Was I appropriately assertive in dealing with dysfunctional or ineffective behaviors, or did I hang back and avoid taking action?

☐ Did I engage in self-defeating thoughts and negative self-talk during difficult moments?

☐ Did I conduct an exit survey to get feedback from participants about how they viewed the meeting?

The Five Rules of Facilitation

The strategies in this book acknowledge that facilitating is a complex and challenging activity in which things rarely go as planned. Consider the following axiom:

> **While some facilitations are simpler than others, there are no simple facilitations.**

This isn't offered to set a negative tone, just to remind us all that whatever can go wrong, might just do that. It's a reminder that anticipating and preparing to deal with challenging situations is far better than ignoring them and being surprised when they crop up.

To be better able to anticipate challenges, it's important to understand the potential sources of complexity and the corresponding facilitation rules.

1. The Context: This is the organizational and cultural context that serves as the backdrop to the facilitation. This includes the history of the organization, its relative level of turbulence or stability, its current goals and strategies, its financial health, and its relationship with key stakeholders, plus various cultural elements such as dominant leadership style, the degree of empowerment given to employees, and trust levels.

Failure to do sufficient research into the context is a major source of facilitation failure. It leads to mistaken assumptions and hidden agendas that surface midstream to derail progress. A facilitation design that worked for one client will probably not work with any others. This rule reminds us that we must always do our homework to ensure that the work we do fits the situation and the needs of the client.

> **Context, context, context.**

The First Rule of Facilitation

2. The Purpose: This is the reason for the meeting. It refers to the overall purpose of the gathering, plus the expected outcomes associated with each individual agenda item. Failure to properly define the purpose and identify expected outcomes virtually guarantees a confusing meeting.

No matter how clearly the content or task has been described and communicated, it's simply astonishing how easily the focus of any discussion can change midstream. It's equally astonishing that there always seem to be people in every meeting who are either confused about the purpose or who have a different view of the purpose. This rule reminds us that facilitators can't clarify the purpose early enough or often enough to make sure everyone is still on the same page.

Keep the purpose crystal clear.

The Second Rule of Facilitation

3. The Process: This is the series of steps that will be used to achieve the meeting goal. It also refers to the specific tools and techniques that will be applied. The process can be designed only after the context has been examined and the purpose and the expected outcome have been identified.

Discussions that lack process or where the process is ignored inevitably turn into unstructured dialogues in which thoroughness and objectivity lose out to personal opinion and power plays. In many situations dysfunctional behavior is not the cause of ineffectiveness, as much as it is a symptom of poor process.

Even when a meeting is carefully planned, a myriad of factors can create the need for on-the-spot redesigning of key process elements. This rule reminds all facilitators that they must have a process in mind before setting out.

Always create a detailed process agenda to guide your work.

The Third Rule of Facilitation

4. The Behaviors: This is about how people interact, their intent, skills, and interaction style. It relates to whether or not the members exhibit effective task and maintenance behaviors during discussions.

While there are individuals who are personally dysfunctional or who intentionally disrupt proceedings, a great deal of dysfunctional group behavior is actually the result of poor process. The other major contributing factor is a facilitator who stands by while things fall apart.

Too many facilitators interpret their neutrality about the topic under discussion to mean they should remain neutral about how people act. It's both appropriate and necessary for all facilitators to make interventions to ensure that people's behaviors remain effective at all times.

Don't hesitate to make needed interventions.

The Fourth Rule of Facilitation

5. The Facilitator: This is about what we bring, what we project and how we act. It's our body language, the words we choose, our style in front of the group and the attitude we convey. It's about being a model for the collaborative spirit.

No matter how many tools and techniques you master, no one can be truly effective if they project negative images. Of these none is more detrimental than operating out of a sense of personal importance. Facilitators who use process work to make themselves look important or to exert their influence over outcomes are doing a disservice to the people they lead.

All truly advanced facilitators are authentic, unobtrusive and sensitive. Their main goal is to help groups find their own voice and achieve outstanding results. They realize that tools and techniques are important, but that the most significant ingredient is often the positive presence of the facilitator.

You are the instrument!

The Fifth Rule of Facilitation

While some facilitations are simpler than others, there are no simple facilitations.

The First Rule of Facilitation .... Context, context, context.

The Second Rule of Facilitation .... Keep the purpose crystal clear.

The Third Rule of Facilitation .... Always create a detailed process agenda to guide your work.

The Fourth Rule of Facilitation .... Don't hesitate to make needed interventions.

The Fifth Rule of Facilitation .... You are the instrument!

Notes

2
The Complexities of
Decision Making

HELPING GROUPS MAKE HIGH-QUALITY DECISIONS is a critically important facilitator role. Unfortunately, it's also fraught with complexity. All experienced facilitators know that even an effective meeting can suddenly become deadlocked and end up in a circular debate.

There are so many things that can derail a decision process that it's impossible to list them all, but here are some of the most common decision dilemmas that facilitators encounter. For elaboration on each dilemma, see the page reference to the right.

Decision Dilemma #1: page 48

As discussion unfolds on a particular topic, it becomes evident that group members are struggling to arrive at agreements about things where no decision is actually needed. They may be getting stalled, for example, arguing about the order of items on a list, when the order is actually irrelevant. Or they may be assuming that they all need to agree with an item before it can be written on the flipchart, while the actual purpose of the discussion is simply to list ideas for later sorting. In these examples, group members are confused about whether they're supposed to be making decisions or not.

Decision Dilemma #2: page 53

Midway through the decision-making process, it becomes evident that no one knows if the group actually has the authority it needs to implement its decision. Some members think that they do, while others are certain the decision is ultimately going to be made elsewhere. This causes people to become confused and disillusioned.

Decision Dilemma #3:

Shortly after a topic or issue has been named, there's a debate about how to make the decision. Some people think the item is very important and complicated, so they want to take part in lengthy deliberations. Others have the opposite view and propose a faster process such as delegating the decision to one person or taking a vote in order to move on quickly.

Decision Dilemma #4:

As soon as a topic or issue is described, someone in the group declares that they have *the* correct solution and start to promote it passionately. This sparks someone else to declare an opposing proposition that they then proceed to sell to the group. The two people become totally engrossed in promoting their idea, and listening goes out the window. Other members of the group become positional and take sides. Things get emotional as the meeting becomes competitive.

Decision Dilemma #5

Rather than take a stance that runs counter to an emerging group opinion or that contradicts a proposal made by the leader, group members withhold their opinions. To stay safe, dissenters remain silent and go with the flow.

Decision Dilemma #6:

After much discussion, a consensus statement is finally crafted that seems to express something that all group members can live with. Out of the blue, at the very end of the conversation, one member announces that she can't accept the group decision. In frustration, other members start to badger the objector to conform.

Shifting Group Focus from "What" to "How"

Before we address the previously mentioned dilemmas, facilitators need to be aware that the key to managing these situations often rests in refocusing the attention of the group away from the *content* conversation, where the decision dilemma is taking place, engaging the members in a *process* conversation.

Switching the focus from *what* to *how* changes the dynamics of the discussion. Deliberating on the process elements is much easier since it's a far more neutral topic. It also breaks the pattern of disagreement that may have emerged on the content side. While people may have disagreements on the process side as well, these are generally less heated, and people have fewer rigid positions about the process elements. Once there's clarity about the decision-making process, it will be much easier to help group members make an effective decision.

"Let's stop this conversation and spend a minute talking about how we're going to tackle this item."

"I propose we brainstorm a list first, then sort that list to identify the best ideas."

The solutions to the six dilemmas, described on the following pages, all demonstrate this strategy of refocusing attention to the process in order to get the decision-making activity back on track.

Decision Dilemma #1:

Lack of Clarity About Whether the Group Is Making Decisions

As discussion unfolds on a particular topic, it becomes evident that group members are struggling to arrive at agreements about things where no decision is actually needed. They may be getting stalled, for example, arguing about the order of items on a list when the order is actually irrelevant. Or they may be assuming that they all need to accept an item before it can be written on the flip chart when the purpose of the discussion is simply to list ideas for sorting later. In these examples group members are confused about whether they're making agreements or not.

"I think we're just sharing information!"

I think we're supposed to make a decision!"

Facilitators need to be aware that all conversations can be divided into two categories: those in which decisions are being made and those in which decisions are not being made. Skillful facilitators always know which type of conversation is being conducted and the tools associated with each:

Decisions are not being made in conversations during which members are:

- sharing information
- reviewing data
- giving updates
- making lists

     using techniques like:

- facilitative listening
- brainstorming
- paper brainstorming
- listing ideas, options or criteria for later sorting

Decisions are being made in conversations during which members are:

- formulating joint plans
- finding solutions to problems
- defining member relationships

     using techniques like:

- voting
- multivoting
- decision grids
- building compromise positions
- forging summary statements

Non-decision-making discussions are *I* conversations, so named because everyone is simply stating what they think.

In non-decision-making discussions the facilitator may bounce an idea around the group to build synergy, but largely records individual thoughts.

If there are no decisions being made, it's okay to record the ideas of separate individuals:

"Just shout out your ideas and I'll record them.

I conversations are faster, easier, and less contentious since people are not engaged in reaching agreement.

Decision-making discussions are *We* conversations, so named because members are combining their ideas to create a shared opinion, solution, or plan.

In decision-making discussions the facilitator bounces ideas around to get people to build on each other's thoughts so that what's recorded represents group ideas.

If decisions are being made the facilitator needs to foster a multidirectional conversation:

What can you add to that point?"

We conversations are slower, more difficult, and potentially contentious since people are linking and harmonizing their ideas.

How to Tell If It's a Decision-Making Conversation

You can determine the difference between these two types of conversations by asking members:

In this next discussion do you need to make decisions or will you simply be sharing information?

Why This Is Important

Once you've identified whether a conversation is *I* or *We* oriented, you can more easily select the right process tools. When you're clear about the difference between these two basic types of conversations, it allows you to identify the places where it's advantageous to switch from a contentious *We* process to a less difficult *I*-centered activity. Here are two specific examples:

Decision Deadlock Scenario

A group of eight people is trying to write a two-sentence mission statement. Members are arguing about the order of the words and word-smithing phrases. People get emotional and the conversation spins in circles.

The facilitator stops the action and switches to an *I*-centered technique; namely, inviting everyone to call out the key words and phases they feel should be included and recording these words randomly.

The facilitator then invites group members to help make another list of the values and images that need to be conveyed by the mission statement. This is also a non-decision-making conversation.

Group members are then asked to keep the list of values and images in mind as they use multi-voting dots to rank the key words in terms of their importance to the mission statement. Once the dots are tallied and the words have been prioritized, the task of crafting the two-sentence statement is delegated to two group members as homework for later ratification by the whole group.

Decision Deadlock Scenario

Group members begin to take sides the moment an issue is named. Half of the group want proposal *A*; the other half favor proposal *B*. Neither side is really listening to each other's views; members passionately describe the virtue of their favorite proposal. Since no one is really listening, people repeat their points, and discussions go in circles.

The facilitator stops the stormy discussion about the two proposed solutions and engages the group in a brainstorming activity to identify a list of the critical success factors in any solution.

Multivoting is then used to rank the relative importance of the criteria. Top-ranked criteria are given a greater weight. The criteria are used to construct a decision grid.

Each group then presents the proposal they favor by explaining how it matches the criteria. People who favor the opposing approach are limited to listening and asking clarifying questions. At the end of each presentation, the other party offers a summary of what was presented. No one is allowed to refute or argue points.

Once both proposals are understood, each member privately rates both proposals using a secret ballot. Results are tabulated and brought back to the group for ratification.

In both of these examples the facilitator acted quickly to interject *I*-focused, non-decision-making techniques like brainstorming, multivoting, and a facilitative listening dialogue when attempts to achieve group consensus through shared group discussion bogged down.

Take Another Look at All of Your Processes!

The difference between decision-making and non-decision-making conversations can also be applied to any process. In the modified forcefield analysis conversation illustrated below, a group is being asked to debrief a past experience, project, or program, then identify solutions that all can live with.

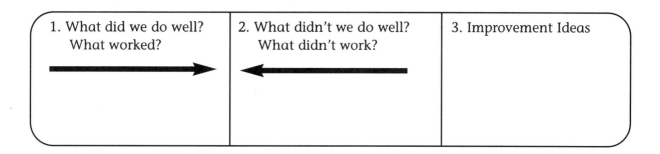

At first glance it would appear that each of the three questions is a decision-making question in which all members need to be able to live with what's decided by the group. In actuality the discussions in columns one and two are non-decision making in nature. These two columns can simply be lists that include points that single individuals think are important. Only the third column is decision making in nature since it must represent the improvements that will be implemented by the group.

It's important to note, however, that even in column three, a noninteractive approach to decision making can be taken by having people simply brainstorm potential solutions for later ranking using multivoting or a decision grid.

To summarize:
- Analyze each conversation to identify if decisions are being made or not.
- Assess which parts of decision-making discussions have the most potential to become contentious or deadlocked.
- Build a design that substitutes individually focused decision-making approaches in these places.

Decision Dilemma #4:

Use of Positional Processes

One of the most prevalent decision blocks happens when one or more people propose a course of action and views become polarized. As soon as a topic or issue is described, someone in the group declares that they have *the* correct solution and start to describe it with passion. This sparks someone else to declare an opposing proposition that they then proceed to sell to the group. The two people become totally engrossed in promoting their ideas and listening goes out the window. Other members of the group become positional and take sides. Things get emotional as the meeting becomes competitive.

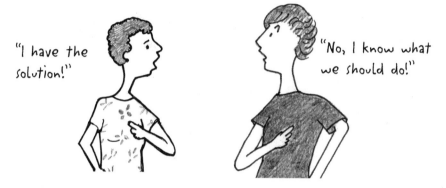

In these cases people take sides. Parties spend their time expounding on the virtues of their idea. No one listens to the other alternative being proposed, so people feel that they need to repeat themselves. As this proceeds, behaviors deteriorate. Arguments emerge. Views become entrenched and relationships may be strained.

Facilitators need to be aware of this all-too-common dynamic because it can emerge in any meeting and always leads to a deterioration in member behaviors. Attune yourself to recognizing this conflict-promoting pattern and be ready to stop polarized discussions by choosing one of two alternate routes:

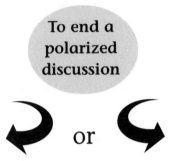

To end a polarized discussion

or

Engage the members in identifying the key criteria for judging each proposal.

Ask members to put their solution aside.

Place these into a decision grid.

Engage the group in clarifying the issue or situation.

Enforce facilitative listening to ensure each party nears the opposing views.

Facilitate analysis of the current situation.

Help members brainstorm possible alternatives.

Engage individuals in using criteria to rate each proposal to arrive at a course of action that everyone can live with.

Use a decision grid or criteria-based multivoting to arrive at a course of of action that everyone can live with.

For more on overcoming positional debates see page 120 in Chapter 3.

Decision Dilemma #5:

The Presence of Group Think

One of the major causes of ineffective decision making stems from what is known as *group think*. This happens when people feel that they should hold back their true feelings out of fear of repercussions. When group think gains a foothold, the fallout is that people withhold their best ideas, dooming the group to faulty decision making and conventional thinking.

Rather than take a stance that runs counter to an emerging group opinion or that contradicts a proposal made by the leader, group members withhold their opinions. To stay safe, dissenters remain silent and go with the flow.

Facilitators must be aware of the natural inhibition against speaking out, especially within hierarchies. This is especially prevalent if any of the following factors are in play:

- The culture of the organization is highly rank oriented.
- Leadership styles are authoritative or directive.
- There's no active practice of feedback activities.
- People have little or no experience with creative thinking or problem solving activities.
- People feel insecure about their industry and their jobs.
- There's a history of conflict in the group.
- There are old, unresolved interpersonal conflicts between members.

Facilitators always need to ask questions about group think when assessing the client's decision-making culture. This involves asking such questions as:

To what extent do people in this group feel free to speak their minds?

Have there ever been repercussions for people who oppose a group opinion or idea proposed by a leader?

Are dissenting views seen as positive or negative by members of this group?

Strategies to Overcome Group Think

There are two main strategies for overcoming group think: setting a climate that fosters openness and selecting discussion techniques that create anonymity or promote objectivity.

Strategies that foster openness

Raising leader awareness about how their presence influences decision-making

Coaching leaders to behave less authoritatively and be more open when receiving input

Providing awareness training about group think using a video that shows group think in action.

Engaging group members in setting norms that encourage openness:

> Before we start today, let's define group think and identify strategies to overcome it.

Praising people who offer honest input and reinforcing that opposing ideas are valuable

Tools that promote objectivity

Using discussion partners and small groups instead of the total group

Using nonverbal brainstorming instead of the verbal version

Identifying a set of criteria with weights, then using those criteria to assess a proposal

Using forcefield analysis to surface both the pros and cons of a proposal:

> Just to insure we're being thorough, let's look at both the pros and cons of this proposal.

Engaging members in a conversation to identify best case/worse case outcomes

Decision Dilemma #6:

Lack of Techniques to Overcome Blocks to Agreement

After much discussion, a consensus statement is finally crafted that seems to express something that all group members can live with. Out of the blue, at the very end of the conversation, one member announces that she can't accept the group decision. In frustration, other members start to badger the objector to conform.

This is a common dilemma in many consensus processes, especially if the stakes are high. Sometimes there's a problem with the proposed solution. At other times, individuals may deliberately hold back their comments only to raise their objections at the last minute.

If a group is being blocked from reaching a consensus because of member objections or concerns, rather than abandoning the emerging solution, apply a technique known as *"Gradients of Agreement."*

Begin by drawing the *"Gradients"* scale on a flip chart. Describe each point on the chart and ask people to identify where they think they are in relation to the emerging decision.

Indicate how you feel about the emerging decision:

1	2	3	4	5
I'm totally opposed and have major philosophical differences with the solution.	I have several serious reservations about the proposed solution.	I have one or two reservations about the proposed solution.	I can live with the proposed solution.	I am in total agreement with the proposed solution.

(Note that 4 is the point of consensus, *not* 5.)

Once all members have indicated their placement, ask people who placed themselves at 1, 2, or 3 to respond to the following questions*:

Question #1   "What puts you there?"
Question #2   "What would move you to #4?"

The ideas generated by the second question will provide suggestions for how the consensus statement can be amended to make it acceptable to everyone. Facilitate actively to amend the statement until all parties indicate that they're at 4 on the scale. Be aware that the group may need to spend additional time problem solving any major blocks that are identified.

* If openness is a major problem, the rating can be conducted in written form and the group can be broken into subgroups to answer the two questions. This is not as positive as conducting the entire exercise in an open manner, but it may be the only way a group with low trust levels can deal with objectors.

Decision Dilemmas Summary Chart

Use the following cascade of questions at the start of any decision process:

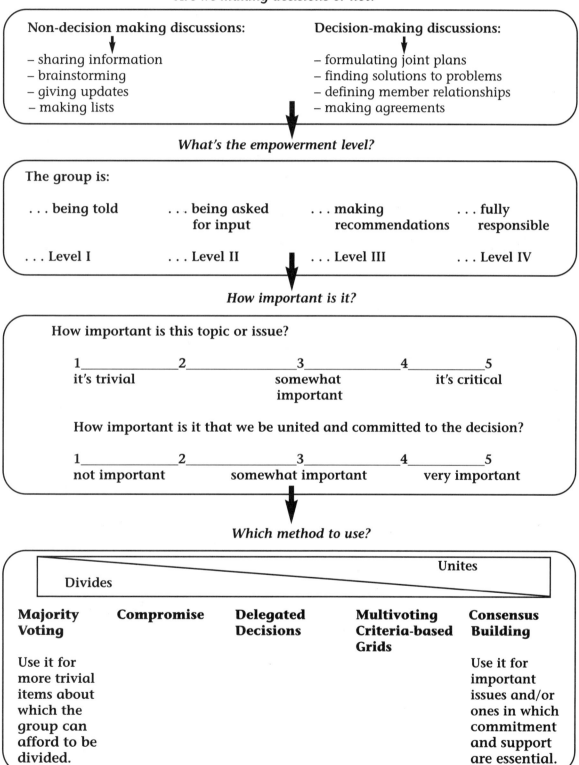

Are we making decisions or not?

Non-decision making discussions:	Decision-making discussions:
– sharing information	– formulating joint plans
– brainstorming	– finding solutions to problems
– giving updates	– defining member relationships
– making lists	– making agreements

What's the empowerment level?

The group is:

. . . being told	. . . being asked for input	. . . making recommendations	. . . fully responsible
. . . Level I	. . . Level II	. . . Level III	. . . Level IV

How important is it?

How important is this topic or issue?

1_____2_____3_____4_____5
it's trivial   somewhat   it's critical
                                    important

How important is it that we be united and committed to the decision?

1_____2_____3_____4_____5
not important   somewhat important   very important

Which method to use?

Divides ————————————————————————————→ Unites

Majority Voting	Compromise	Delegated Decisions	Multivoting Criteria-based Grids	Consensus Building
Use it for more trivial items about which the group can afford to be divided.				Use it for important issues and/or ones in which commitment and support are essential.

More on Decision-Making Options

Whenever a decision needs to be made, facilitators can draw on several methods. Each of these methods creates its own dynamics. Each has pros and cons associated with it. There are also difficulties associated with using each of these approaches. On the following pages is a quick review of the six decision options and some additional strategies to overcome common obstacles.

More on Compromise – It is typically used in situations where there are two or more potential solutions over which people are divided. In compromises people typically make up their minds about the desired outcome at the beginning of discussions. If neither side is willing to accept the solution favored by the other side, a middle position must then be created that incorporates ideas from both options.

In accepting a middle position or compromise, both sides gain some of their points, but both also lose many outcomes that they value. After a compromise, no one feels they actually got what they wanted, so the reaction tends to be: *I'm going to have to live with it!* The result of a compromise is, therefore, something that no one's totally satisfied with.

Since compromise processes begin with solutions already on the table, they tend to be adversarial as parties push for their favorite outcome. While compromise is divisive, facilitators need to be aware that there may be situations where a compromise approach needs to be used. This happens when collaborative efforts fail or when there are two or more known approaches about which the team is divided.

If compromise is unavoidable, the dialogue needs to be structured to minimize its inherent divisiveness. Strategies include making sure that opposing parties hear each other and that both parties look at the pros and the cons of each proposal.

> **Pros** – generates lots of discussion and creates a solution.
>
> **Cons** – lends itself to adversarial debating in which everyone wins, but everyone also loses. Compromise tends to divide parties and often results in damaged relationships.
>
> **Uses** – when it's impossible to achieve a collaborative outcome or when there are clear solutions over which members are divided.

Overcoming Problems with Compromise

If a decision-making activity can't be reframed as a collaborative activity and it becomes necessary to continue with a compromise process, facilitators need to use tools that overcome the main trouble spots**:

Compromise trouble spots	Facilitator strategies
• Individuals are fixated on their solution and don't want to hear about the other position.	• Structure facilitative listening in which each party listens to and then paraphrases the key ideas of the other group.
• People pushing to win.	• Set norms that change the mindset by asking: *"How can we ensure that this decision is a win for both parties?"*
• People emphasize the good points of their own proposal and the negative points of opponent's position.	• Engage participants in a detailed analysis of the pros and cons of both positions or have each party identify only the pros of the other party's idea.
• People become emotional.	• Engage the members in developing decision-making criteria, then use that criteria to objectively screen various options.

Criteria	cost	safety	complexity	reliability	aesthetics	Totals
Option A						
Option B						

Rate each item in each category: 3 = high, 2 = medium, 1 = low

**Note: Also refer to the strategies identified for overcoming polarity on page 57 in this chapter and on page 120 in Chapter 3.

More on Majority Voting – It is a psychological cousin to compromise: both are positional approaches that divide groups into winners and losers. In many ways, voting is the most divisive decision method because it creates a winner-take-all result.

Since majority voting results in winners and losers, the bottom-line in deciding whether to use majority voting is to ask: *Can the group afford to be divided on this issue?* or *Can we live with winners and losers in this situation?* Unless the answer is yes, majority voting should be set aside.

> **Uses** – to make a decision in situations where there are clear choices and where group division is acceptable. Limit use to process and housekeeping matters.
>
> **Pros** – fast, results in a clear decision.
>
> **Cons** – can be too fast and of low quality if people vote their personal biases without the benefit of each other's thoughts. Creates winners and losers, hence divides the group. The "show of hands" method also puts pressure on people to conform.

Overcoming Problems with Majority Voting

Voting trouble spots	Facilitator strategies
• Individuals are fixated on one solution and may not understand the other choice clearly.	• Give each group an opportunity to speak uninterrupted about the merits of the approach they favor. • Ask opponents to paraphrase the main points made.
• People are impatient to make the decision.	• Negotiate for a specific, limited time frame to do a thorough "pros and cons" of each option.
• The vote will cause too large a division in the group.	• Change the boundary of majority to 66% (2/3 of the group).

More on Multivoting – It is a priority-setting tool that's useful when a group has a long list of items that need to be rank ordered. Most people are familiar with the process of voting with stick-on dots, a popular form of multivoting. Decision grids that allow for the numerical assessment of ideas against objective criteria are a form of multivoting.

In contrast to majority voting, which divides the group, multi-voting tends to be neutral; it neither unites nor divides the group. It also frees members from the pressure to agree with others in their party, since multivoting has an element of anonymity. Using objective criteria to guide the multivoting process further ensures a beneficial outcome.

Although multivotes are usually conducted openly, the flip chart holding the list of items being rank ordered may be turned away from the group to minimize the sense of being watched. People can be directed to vote alone or to vote in mixed groups. To limit polarization, it's best not to let all of the members of one party multivote at the same time. It's also a good strategy to ask opinion leaders in the group to multivote last, once all other votes have been registered.

Even though people don't get everything they want in a multivote, the process often results in a consensus. This may be because everyone gets to participate and because all votes count equally. At the end of a multivote, people are thinking: *I didn't get everything I wanted, but my votes counted and I got enough of what was important, so I can live with the outcome.*

> **Uses** – when there's a long list of alternatives or items from which to choose or when applying criteria to a set of options to identify the best course of action.
>
> **Pros** – systematic and objective, democratic, noncompetitive, participative. Everyone wins somewhat and feelings of loss are minimal. A fast way of sorting out a complex set of ideas.
>
> **Cons** – sometimes the optimal solution doesn't rise to the surface because of vote splitting. People may be influenced by each other if the multivote is conducted in the open.

Overcoming Problems with Multivoting

Multi-voting Trouble Spots	Facilitator Strategies
• Leaders vote first and influence or even intimidate others.	• Ask leaders to vote last.
• People vote with different criteria in mind, causing a muddled outcome.	• Establish the criteria of the vote e.g., importance, cost, ease, etc.
• People are afraid to vote in front of others.	• Turn the flip chart to the wall and have people file through one at a time or use a paper ballot.
• People are influenced by how others vote.	• Conduct the multivote by written ballot.
• People have their minds made up before the meeting.	• Facilitate a thorough exploration of the pros and cons of options.
• People vote more than once for their favorite item.	• Set a rule that each person may vote only once per choice.
• People wait until the end and then cast deciding votes.	• Have people file past the board starting with one end of the room or use a paper ballot.
• No one likes the outcome of the multivote.	• Drop the three to five lowest rated items and revote.
• The multivote doesn't yield a decisive outcome	• Assign weights to the dots to create greater numerical differentiation, e.g., 10, 7, 4, 1.

More on Consensus Building – It is a multistage process that begins with the need, interest, or problem that is held in common by all members. It then involves everyone in thoroughly analyzing the relevant facts about the current situation and then jointly developing solutions through a synergistic process like brainstorming to arrive at a mutually agreeable outcome.

Since it's characterized by a lot of listening, open debate, and testing of options, consensus building results in a decision people feel they can live with. Because people work together, it unites the group. Because consensus building unites, the substantive decisions that need to be made by any group should be made using this approach.

Not to be confused with consensus itself, consensus *building* is a systematic process that is characterized by the following steps:

- Discussion is based more on facts rather than feelings.
- Everyone is heard and all opinions are valued.
- A wide range of ideas get shared.
- There is active listening and paraphrasing to clarify ideas.
- Ideas are challenged, not people.
- People build on each other's ideas.
- Rather than pushing for a pre-determined solution, there's an open and objective quest for solutions.
- When the final solution is reached, people feel satisfied that they were part of the decision.
- Everyone feels so consulted and involved that even though the final solution is not the one they would have chosen working on their own, they can *live with it.*

Uses – the only effective decision process for important decisions where the input and commitment of the whole group is needed. The magnitude of the decision being made must be worthy of the time it takes to systematically complete the consensus building process.

Pros – a collaborative effort that unites the group and creates high involvement. Systematic, objective, and fact driven, it builds buy-in and commitment to the outcome.

Cons – time consuming. May sacrifice quality if done without proper data collection or if members lack effective group skills. Requires higher levels of openness and trust than may be present.

Comparing Consensus and Consensus Building

It's critically important that all facilitators understand that facilitation is essentially a consensus-building process. This means that except when facilitators are making lists or recording brainstormed ideas, they are helping group members arrive at agreements that they can all live with. It's also important to know that consensus itself can arise in a number of ways. Facilitators create consensus any time they:

- summarize a complex set of ideas to the satisfaction of all present
- help a group create a common goal into which everyone has input
- gain buy-in from all members to a challenging activity
- link people's ideas together so they feel they're saying the same thing
- help a group to ratify an idea suggested by an outside source
- make notes on a flip chart in such a way that all members feel that they can accept those notes and live with whatever has been recorded

In contrast, consensus building is a complex series of steps designed to create a consensus outcome. This chart helps clarify this important distinction.

> **Consensus (a noun):** the outcome of a decision process that everyone feels they can live with and support. Can arise spontaneously after a multivote or even after a heated argument.
>
> **Consensus Building (a verb):** a series of systematic steps that involve people in working together to objectively search for optimal solutions.

Facilitators should avoid ending a consensus-building exercise by asking:

"Is everyone happy?" or even *"Does everyone agree?"* At the end of even a great consensus process, people have had to make concessions and are likely not getting exactly what they wanted.

Consensus isn't designed to make people happy or have them in 100% agreement. Its goal is to create an outcome that represents the best feasible course of action given the circumstances.

Don't ask: *Do we all agree?*   or   *Is everyone happy?*

Instead ask: *Have we got a well-thought-through outcome that everyone can live with and that we can all feel committed to implement?*

Overview of the Consensus-Building Process

In their broadest outline these steps are as follows:

1. Members allocate an appropriate time slot on the agenda, and a commitment is made to deal with the identified item using a consensus approach.

2. Members are given ample time to do their homework and gather needed information.

3. The facilitator helps the group establish time allocations for each step and asks for someone to act as timekeeper.

4. The facilitator helps the group write a clear statement of the issue under discussion.

5. The facilitator gets the group to identify the desired outcome or goal of the decision process.

6. The facilitator makes sure that there are agreed-to norms in place that define effective member behaviors.

7. The facilitator leads a thorough analysis of the current situation.

8. Assumptions are surfaced and tested. All facts are shared and summary notes are made on a flip chart.

9. After a thorough analysis, the group starts to brainstorm possible solutions. All suggested ideas are recorded.

10. Suggested solutions are evaluated according to a set of criteria created by the group.

11. The final solution is agreed to and a clear course of action is laid out. Members work to create detailed action plans.

12. To ensure that nothing goes wrong, the team troubleshoots their action plan by anticipating all the reasons they may fail to implement key steps.

13. Roles and responsibilities are specified, and a reporting mechanism is created.

14. Plans are made to communicate information to stakeholders.

Overcoming Problems with Consensus Building

Consensus building trouble spots	Facilitator strategies
• time-consuming	• consider group size when estimating realistic time needs
• scale of problem too large for process	• avoid tackling huge issues; break the problem down and work on smaller components
• wrong people present	• identify key stakeholders ahead of time and gain their participation
• poor/missing data	• include a step in the planning process to identify needed inputs
• skipping steps	• stay on track; ask people to write down ideas for later inclusion
• low trust	• consider using small groups or an *"Open Space"* approach; use paper slips instead of open brainstorming, use multivoting in place of debating the merits of various options
• emotional arguing fixed opinions	• enforce facilitative listening so people paraphrase each other; do pros and cons analysis to ensure a balanced review of key ideas
• conventional thinking	• ask people to put on other *hats*; pose challenging questions; set criteria to describe fresh thinking, then use it to judge progress
• blocked consensus	• use *"Gradients of Agreement"*
• vague outcomes	• identify specific outcome measures and a reporting process
• poor follow-through on action plans	• troubleshoot the action plan to anticipate potential derailers

Tools Overview

Climate setting:	– welcoming words – naming issues and concerns – norm development – agenda prioritization – room arrangement and amenities – warm-up exercises
Relationship Building:	– getting-to-know-you activities – norm development – training in effective behaviors – role clarification – negotiating relationships – knowledge mapping – cross training – work planning – negotiating empowerment
Context Setting/ Building Buy-in:	– surveys and interviews – questionnaires – sensing scales – visioning – mission statements – clarifying parameters – goals & specific objectives – benefits/consequences – *What's in it for me?* conversations
Sensing:	– questionnaires – surveys – interviews – pilot tests – sequential questioning – benchmarking – facilitative listening – risk assessment – Delphi method – environmental scans – SWOT analysis – multiple-hat thinking
Analyzing:	– assessing against pre-set performance criteria – cost/benefit analysis – forcefield analysis – gap analysis – cause and effect analysis – fishbone diagrams – story-boarding – questioning – process mapping – environmental scans – benchmarking
Idea Generating:	– brainstorming – anonymous brainstorming – questionnaires – multiple-hat thinking – wandering flip charts – focus groups – surveys
Idea Sorting:	– criteria setting – priority setting – decision grid – affinity maps – multivoting – flowcharts – scatter diagrams – matrix diagrams – run charts – pareto charts
Deciding:	– voting – compromise – multivoting – decision grid – delegating to one person – identifying a compromise solution – building consensus – gradients of agreement

The Decision-Making Roadmap

Decision-making processes fit within a general framework where discussion expands before narrowing to arrive at solutions and actions. Facilitators need to understand that each tool has either a starting, expanding, narrowing, or closing nature so that each can be used in the right place and combined correctly with other tools.

Starting	Expanding	Narrowing	Closing

– context describing
– parameters
– outcomes
– ordering
– generating
   solutions
	– data analysis
	– finding causes
	– checking with
	   stakeholders
		– establish criteria
		– prioritize
		– eliminate
		– evaluate
			– next steps
			– implement
			– follow-up

Tools:
– data gathering
– parameters
– testing
   assumptions
– benchmarking
– visioning
– goal clarification
– output measures
– problem statement
– benefits and
   consequences
– priority criteria
– nominal group
– Delphi method
– risk analysis
– facilitative listening
	– questioning
	– cause and effect
	– fishbone analysis
	– gap analysis
	– SWOT analysis
	– storyboarding
	– process mapping
	– data analysis
	– focus groups
	– multiple hats
	– brainstorming
	– open space
	   statement
	– voting
	– pros and cons
	– compromise
		– criteria setting
		– multivoting
		– decision grids
		– priority setting
		– affinity groups
		– flow charts
		– scatter charts
		– pareto analysis
		– matrix diagrams
		– impact analysis
		– stakeholder vote
		– consensus
			– action steps
			– scheduling
			– assign roles
			– activity tracking
			– outcome
			   monitoring
			– troubleshooting
			– evaluating results
			– rewarding

Decision-Making Checklist

___ Clarify right up front if the purpose of the conversation is to make a decision or not.

___ Review the empowerment level that is operative in relation to that item.

___ Identify the importance level of the topic to the group and whether or not the group can afford to be divided or must be united on that topic.

___ Identify which decision-making method will be used and explain the steps to the members.

___ Call attention to all incidents of polarized decision making and ensure that people are encouraged to listen actively to each other.

___ Facilitate a norming discussion to create the norms to fit the sensitivity or difficulty of the issue being decided.

___ Notice group think and urge people not to fold or just give in if they feel they have important ideas on the matter under discussion.

___ Stick with the process chosen for that topic and avoid skipping steps for the sake of expediency.

___ Be very particular about achieving closure on any decision process before moving on to other topics.

___ Stop the action and make immediate interventions if the discussion starts spinning or behaviors become ineffective.

___ If the group has a history of poor follow-through on action plans, always make time in the agenda for troubleshooting of the action plans to ensure that blocks and barriers are anticipated and to put people on notice that follow-through is being taken seriously.

Decision Effectiveness Exit Survey Elements

Exit surveys are an effective way to help raise awareness about weaknesses in the decision process. Consider including up to four questions on an exit survey aimed at generating improvements.

* All of the following questions use a 1 to 5 scale:

1	2	3	4	5
poor	fair	satisfactory	good	excellent

Q.   How thorough was the decision-making process used at today's meeting?

Q.   How effectively did we use our time?

Q.   How well did people do their homework?

Q.   How good were we at really listening and building on each other's ideas?

Q.   How creative and innovative were the ideas we generated?

Q.   How objective and balanced was our evaluation of various options?

Q.   To what extent was true closure achieved?

Q.   How personally satisfied are you with the final decision?

Q.   What is the quality of the final decision(s) made?

Q.   How doable are our action plans?

Decision Effectiveness Survey

Assess your group's decision making effectiveness by using the following checklist. To what extent is each of the following elements present?

	1	2	3	4	5	
Lack of systematic planned approach	1	2	3	4	5	Clear step-by-step process used
No checking of assumptions	1	2	3	4	5	Thorough checking of assumptions
Overuse of voting; misuse of consensus	1	2	3	4	5	Appropriate use of decision methods
No one builds on the ideas of others	1	2	3	4	5	Active listening by members
People focus on their own ideas	1	2	3	4	5	People hear each other's ideas
Emotionally argue points of view	1	2	3	4	5	Objectively debate different ideas
Never stopping to check the process	1	2	3	4	5	Conducting process checks
No consciousness about time	1	2	3	4	5	Use of time is managed and planned
Passive or lack of facilitation	1	2	3	4	5	Active and assertive facilitation
Some dominate, others are passive	1	2	3	4	5	Full and equal participation
Little gets decided	1	2	3	4	5	True closure
No plans to implement	1	2	3	4	5	Clear action plans

Notes

3
Conflict Management Strategies

WHILE FACILITATORS SHOULD ALWAYS BE OPTIMISTIC and hope that things run smoothly, it's important to be realistic about the potential for encountering difficult situations. It's simply a fact that most facilitation assignments don't go as smoothly as hoped. For a complex set of reasons any meeting can easily turn into an uphill struggle.

When dealing with conflict situations it's important to remember that dysfunctional behavior is often a symptom rather than a cause. People could be acting out for a wide variety of complex reasons:

Problems with the task: Members may be unable to manage the work that they're being asked to perform. They may lack required skills or simply be overworked. The task may be unclear or members may not have bought into the task.

Problems with the process: The approach that is being used may simply not be effective in dealing with the task.

Organizational barriers: The members may lack the empowerment they need to handle the task. There could also be organizational barriers blocking member efforts.

Lack of skills: Group members may lack basic meeting or problem-solving or group decision-making skills.

Ineffective leadership: Some leaders lack group management skills. Others even use their power to deliberately undermine group effectiveness.

Interpersonal conflict: There may be clashes in personality types, past conflicts may have left a residue of resentment, or individuals may have alienated their colleagues.

In this chapter you will see how experienced facilitators look below the surface signs of conflict to identify what's really going on before selecting an intervention approach.

If you've facilitated for any length of time, you've probably already experienced many of the things that can go wrong, including that:

- **Groups often attempt to deal with an unrealistic number of items, which causes members to scramble from topic to topic.**

- **Many meetings are designed without paying adequate attention to the process or exactly how each agenda item will be handled.**

- **Meetings can derail when they lack the guiding help of a neutral facilitator.**

- **Many work groups have never received training on how to participate effectively in meetings, so they exhibit patterns of dyfunctional behavior.**

- **Some individuals who behave well in one-on-one settings act out in groups.**

- **Many managers resist all forms of structure because they feel that it constrains them or inhibits discussion.**

- **Front-line staffers who are accustomed to traditional top-down management styles may not view group decision making as part of their job or may feel they aren't paid enough to perform these functions.**

- **An organizational pattern of downsizing, continual change, and poor follow-through on past initiatives may leave employees cynical and resistant.**

- **The people who request facilitation support often lack a clear understanding of what facilitation is; they actually may end up competing with the facilitator or interfering with the role.**

Operating Under Mistaken Assumptions

As facilitators, we often contribute to meeting problems by operating under mistaken assumptions. Facilitators always want to believe that people come to meetings in a positive frame of mind and that they're highly motivated to do the right thing. In today's high-pressure workplace, however, these assumptions may be unrealistic and naive. That's not to suggest that facilitators should become cynics. It's just that facilitation needs to be tempered with a dose of reality. To assure you're in tune with today's workplace challenges, check to be sure that you *aren't* operating under any of these 10 mistaken assumptions:

MISTAKEN ASSUMPTION #1
People want to be at the meeting.

In most organizations, people are pressed for time and stressed like never before. This means they don't have the time or the energy to sit through meetings that don't yield results. In today's climate, it's wise to assume that the participants are *not* thrilled to be there and need opening activities that create buy-in.

MISTAKEN ASSUMPTION #2
Everyone is clear on the purpose of the meeting.

Even when an agenda has been circulated ahead of time, it's amazing how many people remain confused about the meeting's purpose. To make matters worse, meetings commonly shift focus as they progress, which compounds the confusion. It's best to assume that people *don't* know why they're there and to start with a review of the agenda. During the meeting, it's wise to reconfirm the goal periodically to ensure that group members are still aligned.

MISTAKEN ASSUMPTION #3
**There are no distractions, baggage,
or historical precedents blocking participation.**

Given the amount of turbulence in the workplace, it's important to recognize that people's minds may be elsewhere. If a lay-off, personnel change, or major restructuring is rumored or has been recently announced, people may be deeply distracted or even distraught. In these cases, it's important to start with an activity that lets people vent their concerns before moving into the formal agenda.

MISTAKEN ASSUMPTION #4
**People understand the role and powers of a facilitator
and are ready and eager to be facilitated.**

Facilitation is still a vague and poorly understood concept to many people. If a group's leader is present, members may be confused about how their leader and the meeting facilitator will cooperate without competing. If you're facilitating your workgroup or even if you're an outsider, members are probably wondering what gave you the authority to manage the proceedings. It's wise to assume, therefore, that people need a clear explanation of the facilitator's role and what you'll be doing to support their efforts.

MISTAKEN ASSUMPTION #5

**The people at the meeting are appropriately
empowered to make decisions and act on agenda items.**

People often meet assuming that they're making a decision when the're actually only being asked for their opinion. Other times, groups are asked to deliberate on matters that have already been decided. In either case, group members may end up feeling distrustful and manipulated. Unless addressed, this undercurrent of discontent will reverberate throughout any future meetings. So, it's important that facilitators always clarify the extent of the group's decision-making power and to identify any constraints placed on the decision process.

MISTAKEN ASSUMPTION #6

**There are no political or interpersonal factors
operating behind the scenes.**

While we may imagine that an agenda is accurate, the *real* agenda is often hidden. It's always far safer to assume that there are political or interpersonal elements operating behind the scenes. The savvy facilitator does his or her homework in advance to learn about those undercurrents to avoid being caught off-guard and knows strategies to safely surface hidden motives.

MISTAKEN ASSUMPTION #7

Neutral means unassertive

Too many facilitators act as though their neutrality about the content of the agenda also means they have to stay neutral on the process. The opposite is true: the facilitator should be directive on process issues. Besides selecting the approaches, facilitators also need to point out process problems and to redirect dysfunctional behavior. In other words, effective facilitators know how to be appropriately assertive on the process without compromising their neutrality about the content.

MISTAKEN ASSUMPTION #8

I have to put up with their behavior.

Nowhere is it written that facilitators are expected to suffer abuse at the hands of ill-behaved groups, no matter what their rank or perception of self-importance. All facilitators have the right to expect a high level of civility from everyone. Facilitators also need to know that it's appropriate to walk away from an assignment if a group is excessively dysfunctional and resists all interventions.

MISTAKEN ASSUMPTION #9
I'm experienced; I'll just wing it!

Aside from small, impromptu facilitations, process leaders always need to do their homework and create a detailed meeting design that includes alternative activities. Such preparation instills confidence and offers fall-back strategies if the initial meeting design doesn't work. It's better to have a well-thought-through plan, with options, than to expect to be able to come up with process alternatives in the middle of a meeting on the skids.

MISTAKEN ASSUMPTION #10
It's my fault things didn't work out!

When things go wrong it's very common for facilitators to blame themselves. This ignores the fact that it may be the group that's underperforming or that the meeting goal may have been inappropriate. It's always a better strategy to seek objective feedback and analyze what really went wrong before engaging in self-defeating thoughts that undermine personal confidence.

This list of mistaken assumptions can serve every facilitator as a checklist during the design phase. To help you develop strategies to deal with them, the interventions described later on in this chapter address these various mistaken assumptions as they manifest in specific situations.

The Importance of Making Interventions

Even the best-planned meeting can run into problems. Knowing this, skilled facilitators are always ready to take corrective action. They constantly monitor the group's dynamics and periodically check the effectiveness of the process.

When effectiveness slips, skilled facilitators don't look the other way or pray that problems will vanish if the group takes a break. Instead, they assess the situation and make a timely, appropriate intervention.

> **Definition of an intervention:**
> **Any action taken to improve a situation.**

"Let's stop a minute and see how this is going."

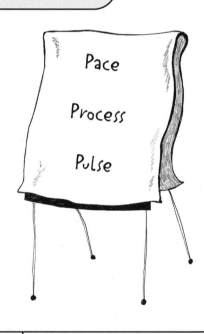

Pace

Process

Pulse

CHECK THE PACE —	**CHECK THE PROCESS —**	**CHECK THE PULSE —**
Ask members about pace:	Periodically ask members whether they feel the meeting design is working:	Watch body language and periodically ask:
"How do people feel about the pace of the meeting?	*"Is the approach we're using working or should we try something else?*	*"How's everybody feeling? How's your energy level?*
Is it dragging or do you feel rushed?	*How else could we do this? Do you think our discussions would benefit from trying . . . ?"*	*Is anyone feeling frustrated, that their points aren't being heard, or that the meeting isn't on track?"*
What can we do to improve the pace?"		

Knowing When to intervene

Regardless of its length and complexity, an intervention is always an interruption. You're stopping the group and drawing people's attention to the process or how the group is functioning. Since intervening disrupts the flow of discussion, it's important to address the issues quickly and return to the discussion at hand.

If you intervened every single time there was a problem, you'd probably be interrupting too often. Instead you need to discern which situations absolutely require an intervention. Below is a checklist to use in deciding when an intervention is appropriate.

Ask yourself:

- How serious is the problem?

- Might it go away by itself?

- What would happen if I did nothing?

- How much time will it take to make the intervention? Do we have that time?

- How much of a disruption will intervening likely cause?

- What impact will it have on group dynamics?

- Can participants handle the intervention given their level of openness and trust?

- How will it affect the flow of the meeting?

- What's the likelihood the intervention might damage anyone's self-esteem?

- What's the risk that the intervention will backfire?

- Do I know these people well enough to do this?

If your answers to the above questions support an intervention, then by all means take action. If an intervention is truly needed, doing nothing will only make the problem worse.

Nine Ways to Intervene

This book covers 30 common facilitation dilemmas from the perspective of symptoms, underlying causes, facilitator pitfalls and intervention strategies. All the suggested strategies are modeled on the principles and core beliefs of effective facilitation and provide strategies for overcoming the 10 mistaken assumptions shared earlier. All of the interventions described are made on the process level to preserve the facilitator's neutral role.

The intervention strategies described fall into nine basic categories. You'll discover that some situations resolve themselves with a single approach, while others require a combination of two or more. Each situation is unique, so you'll need to judge which intervention approach to use, as well as decide on the timing and the order of activities.

INTERVENTION CATEGORY #1 — Context Setting

This type of intervention is appropriate when the purpose, process, roles, and other parameters are unclear or missing.

Intervention activities in this category include creating a vision or clear goal, setting specific objectives, developing milestones or other output measures, clarifying roles and responsibilities, establishing time frames, identifying financial and other constraints, and clarifying decision-making levels:

Vision/goal

Objectives/measureable outcomes

Roles and responsibilities

Constraints: time, budget, scope of work

Within our control/outside our control

Empowerment level/decision-making authority

INTERVENTION CATEGORY #2 — Commitment Building

This type of intervention is appropriate when trust levels are eroded, and individuals are resistant and lack buy-in.

Intervention activities include conducting interviews and surveys before meetings to raise awareness about resistance factors, using rating scales during the meeting to map resistance levels, using forcefield analysis to identify blocks, facilitating partner interviews to encourage venting of concerns, posing buy-in questions that generate commitment, and creating organizational support for initiatives:

Identifying opportunities and obstacles

Venting concerns and issues

Helping people see what's in it for them

Surfacing and working through resistance

Creating organizational support

INTERVENTION CATEGORY #3 — Process Adjustment

This type of intervention is appropriate when the discussion has stalled, and the group is making little or no progress.

Intervention activities include stopping to check if the tool or approach being used is yielding results, testing the current approach, and trying alternative approaches:

Is this approach working?

Are we addressing all of the key elements?

Does everyone feel heard and part of the process?

Are we getting the quality of answer you need?

Should we try another approach?

INTERVENTION CATEGORY #4 — Norm Development

This type of intervention is appropriate when the group lacks the norms it needs to deal with challenging situations.

Intervention activities include asking generic norming questions, posing norming questions in response to specific situations, and using a survey format to test adherence to existing norms such as the one shown below:

To what extent do we listen to others?

1_____2_____3_____4_____5_____

How good are we at remaining objective and open-minded when there's a disagreement?

1_____2_____3_____4_____5_____

To what extent do we stay on topic during meetings?

1_____2_____3_____4_____5_____

INTERVENTION CATEGORY #5 — Behavioral Redirect

This type of intervention is appropriate when ineffective behaviors threaten both progress and group cohesion.

Intervention activities include coaching individuals in private as well as coaching on the spot using a three-part structure:

1) Describing the behavior —   "I'm noticing that . . ."

2) Describing the impact —   "I'm concerned that . . ."

3) Redirecting the behavior —   "I need you to . . ." or
"What should we do . . . ?"

INTERVENTION CATEGORY #6 — Structured Feedback

This type of intervention is needed when the group needs to hear feedback about its performance so members can implement corrective action.

Intervention activities include using a variety of surveys including team assessment instruments, meeting effectiveness surveys, and exit surveys, then using the "Survey-Feedback" methodology to process the feedback:

Reasons for Ratings?	Ideas to Improve

INTERVENTION CATEGORY #7 — Conflict Mediation

This type of intervention is needed when two parties or two individuals are openly engaging in an unresolved conflict that's hampering the progress of the whole group.

The main activity within this category of intervention is to bring the conflicting parties together in private so that they can listen to each other and exchange needs and offers:

What I/we need from you:	What I/we are offering in return

INTERVENTION CATEGORY #8 — Skill Development

This type of intervention is appropriate when group members are missing the key skills they need to debate objectively, make decisions, or implement action.

Intervention activities include conducting a skills needs assessment, observing group process and offering feedback, conducting formal training sessions, providing just-in-time reading materials; and using role plays and coaching sessions:

Skills we have	Skills we need

INTERVENTION CATEGORY #9 — Rapport Development

This type of intervention is appropriate when group members are reserved because they don't know each other or because there's tension in the air.

Intervention activities include using icebreakers, warm-up games, team challenge exercises, and humor. Since warm-up activities need to match the specific dynamics of each situation, no generic examples are provided with the case scenarios.

As you read through the 30 scenarios on the following pages, you will notice that the interventions that are made feature a combination of strategies from the nine categories of activities. While some interventions can be made using activities from a single category, most situations feature a complex combination of challenging elements.

Many people think that humor is the best remedy for resolving difficult situations. If this were true, we would all be having a lot more fun at our meetings!

While humor definitely can warm up a meeting and build rapport, it shouldn't be relied on to resolve serious problems. In fact, using humor instead of a targeted intervention strategy may leave you looking like an ineffective joker.

"Have you heard the one about . . ."

The Art of Positive Confrontation

To new facilitators or those who've had the rare experience of facilitating only harmonious meetings, the interventions on the following pages may seem overly assertive, even confrontational. If you're not used to leading tough conversations, you may find yourself thinking that many of the suggested interventions seem too assertive!

Such a reaction is quite understandable, particularly if the group you're facilitating includes the people you work with or report to! If you share this inhibition, please remember that the purpose of all interventions is to be helpful — never to be mean, combative or punitive. The key to doing this right has everything to do with how you approach it. This includes your intent, the words you use, your body language, and your tone of voice.

If you become angry or sarcastic, or use harsh, judgmental language, then your interventions really will come across as confrontational. Here are a few tips to avoid disastrous consequences:

- Always stay in the neutral, process role; never enter into conflict with group members, even if they attack you personally.

- No matter how others act, stay calm and speak slowly; maintain neutral body language.

- Stay open and friendly, especially toward the person or persons you're redirecting.

- Avoid making judgments about people's motives; never label or blame anyone.

- Continuously express concern for the group and its members.

- Focus on redirecting the situation to restore group effectiveness.

Each intervention described in the following pages includes phrases and strategies to make you effective in dealing with difficult situations, without getting you into trouble or making the situation worse. All of these interventions are built on a two-step foundation:

Step 1   Create awareness of the ineffective situation.

Step 2   Implement actions that improve group effectiveness.

Monitor Your Self-Talk

All facilitators know that sinking feeling when nothing's working and the meeting feels like it's going downhill! During these moments it's natural to panic and start second-guessing yourself. Of course, this is exactly what you shouldn't do. Take a look at your inner scripts. When things go wrong, do you automatically think:

Oh-my-gosh this just isn't working! This is my fault! My design isn't any good. I'm a terrible facilitator. I don't know what I'm doing.

Engaging in such defeatist thinking will only erode your ability to be effective. Instead, focus on how naturally complex and challenging human interactions are. Adopt a new attitude that storming is normal and doesn't mean you're doing a bad job.

The moment negative self-talk starts to creep into your consciousness, replace those thoughts with ones that'll help you make it through the turbulence:

Looks like this isn't working. This sort of thing happens. I need to try something else.

When Nothing Works!

We all need to accept that there are times when nothing works! It's important to recognize these situations and terminate facilitation efforts that have no chance of success. Some of the situations that defy our best efforts include when:

- The people at the meeting have no real intention of resolving the issue on the table or taking the actions being discussed and are simply going through the motions.

- There are one or more constraints, outside the control of the group, that make it impossible to change the situation being discussed.

- Participants are acting with negative intent and are using the meeting as an opportunity to strike out at each other.

- One or more parties are using the meeting to achieve a personal outcome, gain political power, or control a situation.

- The substantive decisions will actually be made behind closed doors and the meeting is simply being used to provide the appearance of participation.

- The participants are using the meeting to continue an unresolved conflict that should be dealt with elsewhere.

- Trust levels are at such low levels that individuals are unable to move forward.

- One or more individuals have personality disorders that require professional counseling.

Finally, remember that you don't have to accept a facilitation assignment that's impossible, dishonest, or disrespectful of you or any other party. State your concerns clearly and inform the person requesting your help that you aren't the right person for the assignment. Exit the scene graciously, and leave the door open to future collaboration under more favorable conditions.

The senerios shown on the pages that follow are 30 concrete examples of the typical conflict situations that facilitators encounter. For each example there is a description of the challenge, an assessment of what's really going on, and a list of facilitator pitfalls and detailed intervention strategies.

1 Role Confusion

"What's a facilitator?"

The Challenge

- Participants ask you who you are and wonder why you're at the meeting.
- If you're a regular member of the group, people are confused about why you're suddenly playing a different role.

"What do YOU think we should do?"

- The leader interjects comments about how the meeting should be run and second-guesses your process suggestions.
- People ask you for your opinion about the topic under discussion.
- Participants are surprised if you stop proceedings, redirect behavior, or intervene in any way.
- People expect you to take responsibility for some or all of the follow-on action steps.

What's Really Going On

- People don't understand what facilitation is or how to use it.
- Since the concept of a neutral, process role is not understood, people assume you're there to offer advice about the topics under discussion.
- External consultants are often seen as people employed by management and tasked with representing management's point of view.
- Individuals who've been in control of the meeting in the past may be reluctant to let you manage the proceedings.
- Some leaders may feel that they'll look powerless if they allow someone else to run *their* meeting.

Facilitator Pitfalls

- Assuming that people know what facilitation is or understand the difference between the process and the content of a meeting.
- Not explaining the role clearly.
- Failing to ask the group for what you need from them in order to be effective in the role.
- Not meeting with the leader ahead of time to define your respective roles.
- Failing to clarify the process whenever confusion about your role surfaces.

Intervention Strategies

- Assess ahead of time whether group members understand facilitation.
- Meet with the leader before the meeting to assess his or her level of comfort with facilitation and to clarify your respective roles.
- Address role confusion at the start of the meeting, with a clear and concise overview of the roles and responsibilities of a facilitator.
- Point out role confusion whenever it resurfaces and immediately refer back to the explanations you provided at the start of the meeting.

Facilitators do . . .
— Suggest ways of proceeding
— Offer tools and techniques
— Make sure everyone is heard
— Point out digressions
— Ask probing questions
— Offer ideas for your consideration
— Offer feedback on the meeting
— Suggest improvement ideas
— Help the group achieve closure
— Encourage clear next steps
— Manage the process so members are free to participate in the discussion

Facilitators don't . . .
— Try to influence your decisions
— Take control away from you
— Make content decisions for you
— Take responsibility for action steps

"Here's what you'll see me doing and NOT doing at this meeting . . ."

*TIP
During any meeting, be on the look out for signs that people might be getting confused. It's a good idea to periodically ask members if they'd like you to review your role again.

2 The Personal Attack

"Who are you anyway?"

The Challenge

- Soon after you introduce yourself, someone brazenly asks you who you are and what gives you the authority to lead the meeting.
- The objector may say that an outsider can't possibly know the organization or its people well enough to manage an important meeting.
- In really confrontational situations group members may even challenge you personally or your qualifications.

"You're not an expert in our field!"   "You're not from this organization."

"You don't know us!"

What's Really Going On

- Participants may have a valid concern that you aren't qualified to handle the discussion, especially if it's highly technical in nature or has a sensitive history.
- Group members may be confused about the role of facilitator and are assuming that you'll be involved in making decisions.
- A controlling person in the group may be challenging your authority because they're traditionally at the front of the room.
- Someone may decide to put pressure on you to test your ability to deal with conflict.

Facilitator Pitfalls

- Taking offense and becoming emotional.
- Telling the objector that you're personally offended.
- Becoming defensive by launching into a detailed recital of your experience and qualifications.
- Using the names of people in power to bolster your position.
- Agreeing that you have few skills or qualifications.
- Breaking down and resigning on the spot.

"I've done this before!"

"I've got a Ph.D.!"

"I know your C.E.O!"

Intervention Strategies

- Remain totally calm and do not respond to a challenging comment even if it's a direct question.
- Ask people to repeat their objection so that they're forced to own it and hear just how awful it sounds.

"Please repeat your concern again so that everyone can hear it."

"I said, I didn't think you were qualified to run this meeting."

- Ask for more details so that the objector has to explain what he or she means. Say something like: *"Please tell me exactly what your concern is."*
- Validate the comment, and thank the objector for bringing it to the attention of the group; this will make you that person's champion and, most likely, make the objector feel guilty for having attacked. Calmly say something like:

   "Thanks for being so brave. You could be right about my not being qualified or not knowing this group."

- Now place the ball back in the objector's court by asking him or her and the group:

   "What do you need to know about my qualifications to feel more confident about me?" and/or *"What additional background information can you share?"*

- Offer details about your education and experience *only* after group members have directly asked you for them.
- If the problem stems from a lack of clarity about the role of the facilitator, clarify your role as process leader.
- You can often put an end to a direct challenge by repeating the original concern and then postponing the issue by saying something like:

   "You may be right about me not being the right person for this job. How about parking your reservations about me until midway through this meeting. Then we'll stop and assess whether or not this is an effective session."

*TIP

Never respond to an attack with a detailed defense. Instead put objectors on the spot by making them describe their objection and asking them to help identify solutions.

3 Lack of Authority

"You can't facilitate me!"

The Challenge

- The person who requested your assistance asks participants to give you their total support, but some group members ignore this request.
- People exhibit negative body language; e.g., turning their back to you.
- Participants challenge your process suggestions or try to change the flow of the meeting.
- People talk about their rank, mention the names of absent senior level managers, or try to sound authoritative to intimidate you and others at the meeting.
- When you propose a specific tool or time frame for a discussion, group members start to debate your proposals.

What's Really Going On

- The group may have some high-status members who are rank conscious and accustomed to being in charge.
- The members may be inserting you into their internal pecking order.
- Members may view you as having a much lower rank than they have, so they see no reason to listen to you.
- If you're unknown to the group, you may not have had time to establish your credibility.

What am I doing here? I can't deal with this level of people!

Facilitator Pitfalls

- Failing to understand that any group will give you the power you need if you demonstrate that you're skilled and capable of helping them.
- Failing to negotiate the power you need at the start of the session.
- Allowing yourself to feel intimidated and letting the group undermine your role.
- Engaging in defeating self-talk that erodes your confidence.

Intervention Strategies

- Use positive self-talk to stay calm and assured.
- Clarify the role of the facilitator.
- Point out that facilitators have no power beyond that which is given to them by the group.

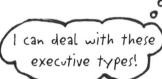

I can deal with these executive types!

- Point out the anticipated challenges of the meeting and ask group members to grant you specific powers:

  "Think about all the things that could make this meeting difficult. What would you want me to do if discussions go off-track or disagreements become heated? How can I make sure we are hearing from everyone? What should I be able to say or do if the meeting becomes ineffective?"

- Ask members to set clear limits on their own power:

  "We have some very senior people here. This can limit discussion and intimidate participants. What can you do to minimize this effect? How can we make sure that ranks and titles get left at the door?"

- If the group fails to offer you authority, ask the group directly for what you need from them. Write your needs on a flip chart. Review your list of needs, and ask the members for their commitment to each item. Post the agreed-to commitments in clear sight, and hold the group accountable for them.

"Here's what I need to ensure that this meeting is effective . . ."

Facilitator Needs . . .

— I need you to adhere to my process design

— I need to feel free to point out problems with the process

— I need to be able to point out digressions

— I need you to hear and accept my feedback

— I need to be able to intervene in case people argue emotionally or engage in other ineffective behaviors

*TIP

If possible, talk to senior people privately about the group's tendency to resist your facilitation and ask them directly for their support.

4 Unclear Meeting Goal
"What's this about?"

The Challenge

- The meeting agenda lacks a clearly stated goal.
- People seem confused about the purpose of the meeting.
- Several people say that the agenda doesn't match their understanding of the reason for the meeting.
- Some of the participants say they feel they shouldn't be there.

"I thought this was about new software!"

"I thought this meeting was about the budget!"

"I thought it was about work planning!"

What's Really Going On

- There's no clearly stated purpose or goal for the meeting.
- No agenda was circulated before the meeting.
- Participants had no input and/or little opportunity to prepare.
- As the meeting gets started, additional agenda items are tossed on the table.
- Some people are wondering if they really should be there.
- Key stakeholders who should be there aren't present.

"Time's a wastin' . . . Let's just start and see what happens."

Facilitator Pitfalls

- Ignoring the concerns expressed by group members.
- Shutting down anyone who expresses confusion.
- Forging ahead with a disjointed agenda.
- Encouraging people to just go along with it.

Intervention Strategies

"It sounds like there's some confusion about the meeting goal. Let's hear what each of you expected it to be."

- Start each meeting by making a clear statement of the overall goal of the meeting and by reviewing the individual agenda items.
- If a sense of confusion and/or differences of opinion persists, engage group members in a conversation about the meeting goal:

  - Help the group identify a clear goal for the meeting by asking:

    "If we were to have a totally productive meeting today, what would we leave here having accomplished?"

- If there are a number of different goals proposed, clarify each of these and conduct a multivote to identify which goal has priority and each topic's time requirements:

Goal for Today's Meeting	Priority*	Time Needed*
To create clear project parameters		
To delegate roles and responsibilities		
To arrive at a detailed action plan		

* Voting criteria: 1 = Low, 2 = Med, 3 = High

- Use the results of the multivote to refocus the agenda.
- Refer lower priority items to future agendas.
- Help the group identify who needs to be present and excuse people from those portions of the agenda that don't relate to them.
- Stay vigilant for people deliberately shifting the focus of the meeting to their favored goal and point this out by saying:

  "I notice that we have just drifted onto an item we parked. Let's stay focused on the items being discussed."

*TIP

Unless you've interviewed each group member in advance of the meeting, it's a mistake to assume that everyone is clear about the purpose of the meeting.

5 Agenda Overload
"We're going to discuss all that*!?!"*

The Challenge

- The meeting agenda is vastly overloaded.
- Some of the time frames set by group members are totally unrealistic.
- Some of the items on the agenda, like sharing memos and updates, should be accomplished via e-mail or other formats.
- Some of the agenda items have to wait until other items get resolved.

Facilitator Pitfalls

- Failing to provide the group with an effective meeting structure
- Going along with the demand to lead a badly overloaded meeting.
- Failing to help the group identify the overall goal of the meeting.
- Allowing the group to plunge into an obviously overloaded agenda without determining the priority of each item.
- Failing to point out more effective ways of handling some items outside of the meeting format.
- Facilitating rushed and incomplete decisions because the group insists on pressing ahead.
- Failing to do an exit survey after each meeting or failing to conduct a periodic meeting effectiveness survey in order to prompt the group to make improvements.

What's Really Going On

- The group members may be under extreme time pressures and feel the need to deal with all of their major issues at their single weekly meeting.
- There may be no specific goal for the meeting against which to assess whether an item is a priority.
- There may be a pattern of dragging items from previous overloaded meetings onto the next agenda.
- Group members may be inexperienced and unaware of how long complex discussions will actually take.
- Some items on the agenda may be better handled by a sub-group.
- Meetings are too rushed to get to resolution on important items, which compromises the group's continuity and accountability.

"Oh well, let's see how far we get!"

Intervention Strategies

- Do pre-meeting research to determine past meeting patterns and to find out which issues are most important to the group.
- Begin each meeting with a clear goal and a set of specific objectives that describe what the group wants to achieve at the meeting.
- Help group members develop targeted norms to overcome their tendency to overload the agenda by asking specific questions about agenda size:

"It seems that past agendas have gotten overloaded."

"Let's talk about why this happens and what we can do to ensure it doesn't happen again."

- List all agenda items on a flip chart with two columns. Make sure that everyone knows what each item is. Then conduct a multivote in which participants rank each item's priority and time needs as high, medium or low.

- Ensure the group stays on track and on time. Record all off-track topics on a "Parking Lot" sheet.

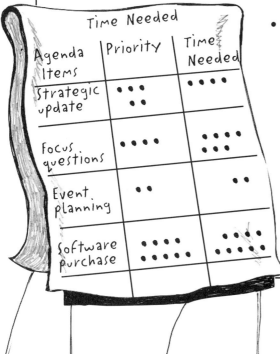

- Intervene immediately if group members introduce new topics, saying:
  "I notice that you've introduced a new topic that isn't on our agenda. I'm concerned that this is going to keep you from achieving your objectives today. Let's park that item and decide its priority at the end of the meeting."

*TIP
Agenda overload is the root cause of many meeting dysfunctions. Prioritizing helps people prepare and insures that the right people attend.

6 Mistaken Assumptions
"Who told you that?"

The Challenge

- As soon as you've finished reviewing the meeting objectives and agenda, people look puzzled and start to question agenda items.
- Various people have different opinions about the underlying facts of the situation and start to argue.
- As the meeting progresses, you notice that there are lots of side-chats and passed notes.
- People look confused and frustrated.
- Meeting discussions go in circles and fail to yield results.

What's Really Going On

"Who told *her* we needed training?"

"Doesn't she know we already did this?"

- The agenda is based on incorrect information about the situation or the needs of the group.
- Important information may have been suppressed in advance of the meeting.
- People may have deliberately offered misleading information to exert control over the agenda.
- You may have been told certain facts to shape your opinion about the meeting outcome or one of the participants.
- The underlying facts of the situation may be sensitive and beyond the coping ability of group members.
- People may know what's going on behind the scenes but be unwilling to discuss the situation openly.

Facilitator Pitfalls

- Failing to do adequate research.
- Asking the wrong questions or interviewing the wrong people.
- Not stopping to test assumptions at the start of the meeting.
- Failing to pay attention to body language or asking people what their body language means.
- Pushing ahead with the prepared agenda out of fear of looking ineffective or losing control.
- Lacking the skills or techniques that safely bring out hidden assumptions and encourage people to surface them.

Intervention Strategies

- Conduct interviews with a wide range of people, including key stakeholders who are external to the meeting group.
- Use an anonymous survey to solicit more candid data.
- Know the right questions to ask in order to surface assumptions during interviews. These include tactful questions about:

- Identify your assumptions and make them explicit either at the start of the meeting or, even better, during pre-meeting communications:

"Before I review the agenda, let me share my key assumptions."

— The history of the situation
— Organizational support levels
— Empowerment levels
— Values, beliefs, and attitudes
— Group cohesion and trust levels
— Personalities and politics
— Objectives and expected outcomes
— Willingness, interest, and attitudes
— Skill levels
— Roles and responsibilities
— Timing and location

- If it's likely that group members won't speak up, ask each person to find a partner with whom to have a private discussion about any changes they would propose to your list of assumptions.

- If trust levels are too low for partner sharing, you could turn your assumptions into a survey posted in a corner; during a break ask people to rate the correctness of each assumption on a scale of one to five. Ask for more information about the low-rated items.

- Learn methods of inquiry that allow you to probe into sensitive issues without threatening group cohesion. The methods include "Third-Party Questions" (What would others say?) and "Magic Wand Questions" (What would be ideal if money were no object?)

*TIP
The best time to check assumptions is before a meeting.

7 Hidden Agendas
"Wish we were talking about the *real* issues."

The Challenge

- The goal of the meeting and the stated agenda items do not represent the real issues facing the group.
- A major issue that is central to the discussion is being avoided.
- Group members assume they have decision-making powers that they actually do not have.
- A group member unexpectedly puts a topic on the table that was not on the agenda.
- During breaks, people are overheard saying that the wrong items are on the agenda.

Wish we were talking about the cutbacks!

We all know the real agenda!

What's Really Going On

- The hidden issue may be seen as too sensitive for an open discussion.
- Group members may lack the trust or skills they need to deal with sensitive issues.
- Management may not trust the group to be involved in discussing certain topics.
- The item under discussion may already have been decided behind closed doors; the meeting is a pretense.

Facilitator Pitfalls

- Failing to conduct one-on-one interviews before the meeting to identify hidden issues.
- Not examining the blocks to identify strategies to overcome them.
- Failing to determine the decision-making authority of the group regarding specific issues.
- Surfacing a sensitive agenda topic without first checking the readiness of group members to deal with it.
- Failing to create a safe environment for confronting sensitive issues.

Intervention Strategies

- Conduct one-on-one interviews with key stakeholders to uncover sensitive or hidden issues.
- Clarify with management which items are within the control of the group and which are outside of their control.
- Clarify the specific empowerment levels associated with each agenda item to determine if, in each case, the group is (see right):

1. Being told an outcome
2. Being consulted for ideas on a matter to be decided elsewhere
3. Being asked to discuss a matter and make detailed recommendations that require management approval
4. Making a decision that they can act on.

Please indicate to what extent . . .

1. We're really making meaningful progress.
1____2____3____4____5
definitely not!   definitely

2. We're dealing with the right issues.
1____2____3____4____5

3. We're being totally honest and open.
1____2____3____4____5

4. We're ready and willing to deal with sensitive underlying issues.
1____2____3____4____5

- Begin the meeting by posting a summary of the operating assumptions and asking which are correct, incorrect, or missing.

- If no one is willing to speak up to identify the hidden agenda, create a survey (see left) that people can complete anonymously at a midpoint in the meeting.

- If the survey indicates that there are sensitive issues that need to be addressed, help group members identify targeted norms that create a safe climate for discussion by asking:

*TIP

It's always important to understand the conditions that need to be in place before hidden items can be safely surfaced and productively dealt with.

"What assurances, conditions, or rules need to be in place before we can safely and productively discuss this issue?"

8 Resistance and Lack of Buy-in
"What's in it for me?"

The Challenge

- When you introduce the topic of the meeting you notice bored looks, eye rolling, and folded arms.
- People shake their heads and give each other sideways glances.
- When you ask for participation you get silence instead.
- If participants do open up, they say things like: *"I'm too busy for this! This is a total waste of time! Nothing ever happens afterwards!"*

What's Really Going On

- People may be overworked and unable to cope with additional responsibilities.
- People may not see any positive outcome for themselves and feel that they're just being asked to do more work.
- The environment may be filled with cynicism and mistrust because past initiatives were inadequately supported or not implemented.
- People may suspect another flavor-of-the-month project.
- Management may have become the enemy, with you standing in as their agent.
- Some participants may sit passively through the meeting, then work behind the scenes to undermine whatever initiative is launched.

Facilitator Pitfalls

- Ignoring the negative body language and just forging ahead.
- Relying on humor to improve how people feel.
- Selling the initiative by pointing out all the good points.
- Giving participants a pep talk about team spirit and urging them to give it a try.
- Getting defensive and mirroring the group's negativity.
- Falling back on your professional credentials.
- Mentioning your connections with people in management.
- Making people feel it's all nonnegotiable and there's no turning back.

This is a great project. You need to give it a chance. You're going to get a lot out of this. Besides, the decision's been made!

Intervention Strategies

- If people are displaying negative body language, report on what you see. Make it okay for people to express their negativity:

    "I'm noticing some folded arms and concerned looks. We all need to know what's on people's minds. Please tell us what this means."

- Listen respectfully to concerns, and paraphrase main points.

- If you sense resistance under the surface, you can draw it out by posting a resistance scale. Ask each person to secretly select where they are on the scale. Assure people that they do *not* have to reveal their ratings.

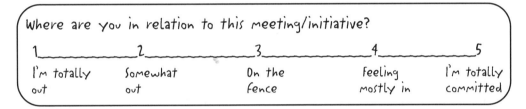

- Once people have secretly identified where they are, pose a question:

    "What would you need to believe was going to be the outcome of this activity before you would move your rating toward 5? What conditions would need to be in place? What supports or assurances would you need?"

- To encourage people to speak up, ask everyone to find a partner so that they can safely reveal their conditions for moving forward.

- Record all the desired outcomes, conditions, assurances, and supports on a flip chart—be careful not to eliminate those that appear to be unrealistic at this point.

- When the discussion is over, review all the conditions for moving forward; during this review ask the group members to assess how realistic each condition is.

- If the conditions for buy-in are complex, like getting a senior manager to join the committee, you may need to facilitate in-depth problem-solving and action-planning discussions for these items.

- Set up an ongoing mechanism, like an entrance survey, to be completed at the start of all future meetings, so that the group can monitor the extent to which their conditions for buy-in are being met.

*TIP
The only effective way to dispense with resistance is to acknowledge it and engage group members in identifying strategies to overcome it.

9 Resistance to Process

"Don't fence us in!"

The Challenge

- The group is resisting all attempts to provide structure to the meeting.
- Sometimes they resist your process suggestions as soon as you introduce them.
- At other times they start out following your suggestions, but quickly revert back to the freewheeling approach they're used to operating with.
- Members insist that their thought processes are so complex that they require a totally ad hoc approach.

What's Really Going On

- The group isn't accustomed to using a structured approach.
- Certain members may feel like they're being asked to give up control.
- The type of participants who thrive on meeting mayhem will feel you're cramping their style.
- Some people may be using chaos to avoid making decisions or taking responsibility.

"We're a very spontaneous bunch!"

"We like it best when ideas are just flowing!"

"Process slows us down!"

- Some people come to meetings to push their views until others give in. These people don't want to follow a structure that makes them look at all sides of an issue or hear others' points of view.
- Senior managers and executives often feel that they're above being facilitated and just want you to act like their scribe.

Oh well, it's _their_ meeting!

Facilitator Pitfalls

- Allowing discussions to take place without any structure.
- Quietly watching as conversations go in circles or veer off track.
- Passively accepting the scribe role.
- Failing to offer feedback or intervene.
- Failing to be assertive about the need for a clear process.

Intervention Strategies

- Clarify that a facilitator is not a passive scribe and outline the roles and powers of a facilitator.

- Acknowledge concerns about using techniques that feel artificial by saying:

    "Most groups don't want to do things that feel gamey and neither do facilitators."

- Bargain for a chance to facilitate properly. Say something like:

    "I'm going to ask you to let me do my job for the first hour. At that point we'll stop and assess if the process feels artificial or limiting. If it isn't working I'll step down and leave you to your own devices."

- Offer feedback to participants whenever they go back to their unstructured approach:

    "I notice that you just switched topics without bringing real closure to the previous item."

- Provide process suggestions whenever they're needed to help restore group effectiveness:

    "Before you move forward, I suggest we bring closure to the previous item and identify detailed action steps."

- If members are being cooperative, stop periodically to remind them that you're sensitive to their concerns about using a structured approach:

    "Let's stop and see how this is going. Are we making progress? Is the structured approach working?"

- If the group insists on proceeding in an unstructured way, point this out to them. Make it clear that, under these conditions, you're not serving as a facilitator; say that you'd be willing to move back into that role if they take a structured approach:

"You seem to want me to just take notes. I'll do that, but I need to point out that I'm no longer really facilitating. I'll gladly resume facilitating again if you ask me to."

*TIP
Sometimes groups will test you to see if you'll stand your ground. Caving in can set the stage for losing the group's confidence.

10 Lack of Norms
"We don't need rules!"

The Challenge

- The group operates without any explicit norms or rules.
- People insist that they don't have time to set rules.
- When asked to create rules, members object, saying things like:

"We've met for years without rules!"

"Rules will only cramp our style!"

"Besides, we all get along!"

What's Really Going On

- Some people may fear that creating rules will limit their power.
- Participants with dysfunctional behaviors will resist anything that's likely to limit their freedom to act out.
- Some people may be concerned that setting guidelines will take too long.

Wish they'd stop interrupting each other and LISTEN!

Facilitator Pitfalls

- Trying to facilitate any group that lacks behavioral guidelines but clearly needs them.
- Failing to use dysfunctional episodes as opportunities to give feedback and ask members to create targeted norms for specific situations.
- Going along with the group's assertion that norms aren't needed.

Intervention Strategies

- Take a firm stand and insist that having a set of meeting norms or guidelines is a prerequisite for conducting an effective meeting.
- Engage everyone in the norming conversation to get each person's input on a core set of rules, then post these in clear sight.
- If group members fail to suggest norms, post two to five specific norming questions, like the ones suggested below. Ask each person to find a partner and allow three to five minutes for partners to create norms. Then gather up and record responses:
- If your attempts to engage the group fall short, provide the group with a basic set of norms. Review them and ask members to ratify them. Then post the ratified norms in clear sight.

"Since you couldn't think of any norms, I'm going to offer these and ask you to ratify them and agree to abide by them for this meeting. I welcome any additions that you think will improve the list."

Meeting Guidelines
— How can we ensure that everyone is heard and that all opinions are valued?
— What do we need to do to make sure there's real closure at the end of each discussion?
— What should we do if the conversation gets sidetracked?
— How can we ensure that we have healthy debates rather than emotional arguments?

Meeting Guidelines
— We will listen to others
— We will respect all points of view
— We will give the meeting our full attention
— We will hone time limits
— We will stay on topic
— We will agree that everything said here stays here

- Use dysfunctional instances as opportunities to develop targeted norms. For example:

"I noticed that the last couple of speakers repeated their points several times. I'm concerned that this may indicate that people don't feel their points are being heard. What rule should we add to the meeting guidelines to ensure that people really get heard?"

*TIP
Remember that you're neutral on content, not on process, so it's appropriate to be directive about creating and using norms.

11 Ignoring Group Norms

"Oh those rules!"

The Challenge

- The group has rules, but they're seldom posted and members consistently ignore them.
- When asked why the rules are ignored, people respond that they're too busy to pay attention to them.

What's Really Going On

- The group has norms but is in the habit of ignoring them; they don't post, refer to, or review them.
- The group may lack training in group or meeting effectiveness skills.
- The group may have entrenched patterns of behavior that certain members don't want to give up.

Facilitator Pitfalls

- Allowing the group to continue to ignore its rules
- Turning a blind eye to dysfunctional behaviors

Intervention Strategies

- Identify which rules are most consistently ignored or violated.
- Turn these items into a survey, and ask group members to rate each item as they leave for a break. This survey also could be used an an entrance survey at the the start of a meeting. (*Note:* If trust levels are too low for an open exercise, create a written survey and tabulate the results for later feedback.)

> ## Exit Survey
> Please respond to the following questions:
> 1) To what extent do we stick to our agenda and stay on track?
> 1 —————— 2 —————— 3 —————— 4 —————— 5
> Not at all   Somewhat   Totally
> 2) To what extent does everyone feel their ideas get heard?
> 1 —————— 2 —————— 3 —————— 4 —————— 5
> Not at all   Somewhat   Totally
> 3) To what extent are differing ideas respected and acknowledged?
> 1 —————— 2 —————— 3 —————— 4 —————— 5
> Not at all   Somewhat   Totally

- Once everyone has rated each question, facilitate a discussion using the "Survey-Feedback" methodology. This involves focusing on one survey question at a time, asking:

	Why did this item get this rating?	What would improve how the group rated it?
#1	→	
#2	→	
#3	→	

- If no one speaks up, ask participants to find a partner to discuss the results, then facilitate a discussion to gather up ideas.
- The items in the right-hand column will either be action steps or new norms. Add the new norms to the group's original set and make sure they're posted in clear sight for the rest of the meeting.

*TIP

Take a firm stand that you can't facilitate a group that doesn't have a clear set of norms that are posted and followed.

12 The Over-Participant
"And furthermore . . ."

"I just have a few more really important points!"

The Challenge

- Individuals who can't limit their airtime.
- People who provide a level of detail that isn't needed or appropriate to the situation.
- Group members who are oblivious to what others want to hear.

What's Really Going On

- Some people have an inflated sense of their own importance.
- Some people simply love to hear themselves talk.
- Dysfunctional talkers are often oblivious to what others need to hear.
- Over-talking may be a ploy to get attention or gain control.

Facilitator Pitfalls

- Not checking with the rest of the group to determine what they need to hear.
- Failing to establish guidelines for presentations.
- Standing by and allowing over-talkers to continue past pre-set time limits.
- Using overly harsh or judgmental language when intervening.
- Coming across as unsure when asking over-talkers to curtail their comments.

"I was wondering if you'd consider stopping soon?"

"Sure, as soon as I finish this last point."

Intervention Strategies

- Help the group set clear time limits for each presentation.
- Appoint one of the group members to act as timekeeper and periodically call out milestones.
- Help the group establish guidelines for each presentation:

  "Before the presentations begin, let's talk about the level of detail people need and some of the specific questions you want to have answered."

- Ask the group to establish a targeted norm at the start of any meeting where you suspect over-talking might occur:

  "We've got a really tight agenda today. What commitments do we each need to make to honor our time-frames?"

- Help over-talkers correct themselves by offering them specific feedback:

  "You've been giving us a lot of implementation details rather than offering an overview of project goals. Please refocus your presentation to be in line with the guidelines we set earlier."

*TIP
This innocent-seeming problem is actually a major cause of meeting ineffectiveness, so don't ignore it. Be prepared to take action whenever it occurs!

- If the over-talker shows no sign of self-control, stop him or her and check with the rest of the group:

  "I'm going to stop you and check with the rest of the group to make sure this is the right time to hear more of your report."

- Firmly point out that the group members are violating their time limits, and clearly state what you want them to do:

  "You're now five minutes over your allotted time. I'm concerned others won't get a chance to present. Please wrap up."

- If none of the above interventions has an impact, take over-talkers aside and give them feedback in a way that encourages them to take responsibility for their actions in future meetings:

  "At today's meeting, you ran over by 20 minutes, even though I asked you to end your presentation twice. This threw the meeting seriously off schedule. I need a commitment from you to ensure that this doesn't happen in the future."

13 The Under-Participant
"I have nothing to add!"

The Challenge

- While some people speak up, others sit in silence.
- When asked if he or she has anything to say, the under-participant declines.
- Sometimes an entire group will sit back and say nothing.

What's Really Going On

- Some people are unaccustomed to attending meetings, let alone being asked to participate in discussions.
- Some people feel insecure about the quality of their ideas.
- Others may feel that their ideas aren't going to be heard or, worse, fear that they'll actually get rebuked for speaking out.
- Participants may be afraid of saying something inappropriate in front of peers or superiors.
- Some people worry that they'll be asked to take part in presentations, role plays, or other activities they think are embarrassing.
- The presence of a senior person may intimidate participants and cause them to shut down.
- The group's over-participants may be shutting down the quiet people.

Facilitator Pitfalls

- Not finding out before the meeting whether people are likely to shut down.
- Failing to find out if the presence of certain people might have a negative effect on participation.
- Assuming that quiet people have nothing to add.
- Sticking with a large group format for most discussions.
- Not setting norms to create safety and comfort at the meeting.
- Leading a discussion in which only the high participators have a voice.
- Forgetting to invite quiet people into conversations.

Intervention Strategies

- Conduct one-on-one interviews with participants to build rapport and determine if people are likely to be open in a group or in the presence of specific senior people.

"Let me tell you what to expect at today's meeting."

- Coach senior people to offer their opinions as questions and suggestions; also, ask them to consider holding their ideas until the end of discussions to avoid shutting down participation.
- Put people at ease at the start of the session by assuring them that no one will be asked to do anything that puts them on the spot.
- Design your meeting around techniques that create safety and get everyone involved. These include having people talk to a partner before giving answers in the large group; using small groups for discussions; using paper slips to gather ideas; and inviting people to write ideas on flipcharts around the room.
- Help the group create targeted norms that encourage open participation by asking:
- Maintain eye contact with the under-participants so they know they're not forgotten and are always welcome to add their views.
- Call on quiet people by name, especially if their body language indicates they may have something to say.
- Find nonthreatening roles for quiet people, like timekeeper, to make them feel valued.
- Encourage under-participants by thanking them for participating.

— How can we make sure that everyone participates and no one dominates?

— What conditions or assurances encourage people to speak freely at this meeting?

— What are those folks who always have a lot to say willing to do to ensure everyone's ideas are heard?

*TIP

Facilitators always need get input from everyone in a group to ensure that final decisions have the full support of all members.

14 The Positional Debate
"I'm right; you're wrong!"

The Challenge

- Individuals become passionately attached to an opinion, then argue emotionally to prove another person wrong.
- People talk over each other, not hearing each other's ideas.
- Individuals get overly emotional and escalate slight differences of opinion until they become battles over principles.
- Some groups have developed an entrenched pattern of splitting into polarized factions as soon as a topic is placed on the table.

What's Really Going On

"I'm right!"

"No, I'm right!"

- Instead of starting with the overall situation and brainstorming ideas, the conversation starts with solutions advocated by individuals.
- People are so engrossed in their own ideas, they aren't really listening to or understanding anyone else's point of view.

- Group members may be unaware of their bad habits.
- The group lacks norms for dealing with emotional arguing.
- Members may lack both interpersonal and group decision-making skills.
- In academic or highly technical circles, analytical individuals may argue endlessly to prove a theoretical point.

Facilitator Pitfalls

- Allowing people to push their positions without offering a process that minimizes conflict and reduces polarity.
- Allowing people to talk over each other or become highly emotional.
- Failing to provide group decision-making skills.
- Failing to make verbal interventions that redirect dysfunctional arguments.
- Saying tentative things like *"It would be nice if you'd listen to each other."*

Intervention Strategies

- Post specific questions that will help the group create a set of targeted norms for managing conflict:

What can we do at this meeting to make sure that people really listen to and understand each other's points?

What should we do if people start to get emotional?

What language is ok/not ok when discussing differences of opinion?

- Encourage effective behaviors by providing training in skills such as active listening and paraphrasing.

- Obtain more power for yourself at the start of a potentially argumentative session by asking:

    "If discussions become argumentative or overly heated during today's meeting, what is ok for me to say or do?"

- If possible, reframe a polarized conflict as an issue or a need; then use a systematic problem-solving approach that gets people working together to analyze the situation and brainstorm joint solutions.

- If you can't avoid letting the group debate two solutions, use a structured approach like a "Criteria-Based Decision Grid" or a "Pros and Cons" approach. These methods will bring more objectivity and balance to the debate.

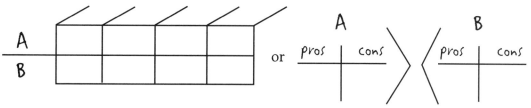

- Throughout the discussion, make firm and clear verbal interventions whenever ineffective arguing breaks out. Use the three-step verbal intervention model:

    1. *"I'm noticing that people are speaking over each other.*
    2. *I'm concerned you aren't hearing each other's ideas.*
    3. *From now on, don't counter until you've summarized the other person's point."*

*TIP

Most of the dysfunctional behaviors that people exhibit in polarized discussions will disappear when you provide more structure and facilitate assertively.

15 The Joker
"Aren't I funny!"

The Challenge

- This is the person who comes to meetings to play the clown.
- No matter how serious the topic, this person tosses out one-liners.
- Group members encourage the joker by laughing and quipping back.

- While appropriate humor helps create a friendly atmosphere, the habitual joker doesn't know when to stop.
- If the joker hasn't bought into the goal of the meeting, he or she will start making fun of the proceedings or even of you:

"I dressed like this because I heard this was going to be a picnic! Looks like you heard the same thing!"

"Your ridiculous comments are getting on my nerves!"

What's Really Going On

- This is a self-appointed role that some people have been playing since childhood.
- Clowns are often trying to cover up how uneasy or excluded they feel.
- If the joker is bitter, the humor can become cutting and destroy trust in the group.
- Jokers often use humor to test authority figures, just like they used it to test their teachers back in school.
- Inappropriate humor is often a power play, deliberately interjected to impede progress and make the group lose focus.

Facilitator Pitfalls

- Letting the joker play havoc with the meeting without intervening.
- Competing with jokers by trying to be funnier than they are.
- Encouraging the joker by giving him or her too much attention.
- Calling on the clown to interject humor in tough moments when a more appropriate intervention is actually needed.
- Using judgmental language or a confrontational tone to shut down the joker.

Intervention Strategies

- Be alert for signs that someone is using humor inappropriately and notice whether others are enjoying the quips or are annoyed by them.
- Be patient and smile the first few times the joker acts out, especially if the quips are harmless and don't interfere with the meeting.
- To call attention to the situation, make a neutral observation to put the joker on notice:

    "I notice that you have an active sense of humor, even during serious moments."

- If clowning around has been a problem at past meetings, engage the whole group in setting targeted norms to curtail it:

- If the joker acknowledges that you're referring to him or her, seize that opening to get him or her to take responsibility:

    "You're talking about me, aren't you?"

    "What can you do to help us stay focused?"

    At the last meeting, having fun seemed to take over and distract us.

    What can we do at today's meeting to make sure this doesn't happen again?

    How can we have a good time without letting humor take us off track?

    What other rules should we set about this?

- Any time jokers use humor inappropriately to harm another person, immediately intervene to get them to rephrase what they said:

    "Why don't you rephrase that comment to take out the humorous spin."

- Another tactic to disarm jokers is to express concern for them personally, while redirecting their behavior:

    "I'm concerned that the humorous spin you're putting on everything is keeping people from hearing your good ideas. Please make your points in a more neutral way."

- If none of these tactics works, take the joker aside for private feedback:

    "I've noticed that you use humor a great deal, even when it isn't appropriate, and sometimes to make fun of other people. This is interfering with the meetings. I need you to be more aware of how you use humor and to limit how much you do it."

*TIP

Don't understimate the power of a joker to make you look like a fool. Excessive clowning around isn't a fun or harmless activity!

16 Side-Chatters

"Psst, Psst, Psst . . ."

"Psst, psst, psst . . ."

What's Really Going On

- Side-chatting that goes beyond the quick sharing of a comment with a colleague is rude and disrespectful behavior.
- Some people do this subconsciously.
- Others mistakenly think that if they're not actively engaged in the topic of the moment, it's ok to conduct a side meeting.
- Some people feel so important that they assume they can do whatever they please, in any setting.
- Side-chatting is often symptomatic of a low trust environment in which people feel reluctant to speak openly.
- Some people may side-chat to test your ability to manage the meeting.

The Challenge

- People chat with those next to them instead of paying attention to the discussion.
- Some of the side-chats are short and respectful, but others are long and disruptive.
- When a serious or contentious item is on the table, some people turn to a colleague and tell them what they really think, rather than share their comments with the group.
- People who are paying attention get angry with the side-chatters for not listening.
- A some point, the side conversations become distracting.

Facilitator Pitfalls

- Ignoring side-chatting, perhaps because high ranking people are doing it.
- Failing to discern if side-chatting is a sign that there's confusion, disagreement, or other hidden problems.
- Allowing a group to meet without norms or meeting guidelines that define effective behaviors.
- Making judgmental or confrontational comments when intervening to end side-chatting.

"I notice that some people have lost interest in the meeting!"

Intervention Strategies

- Help the group create a balanced set of norms or meeting guidelines that help them control side-chatting.

- If side-chatting starts to become a problem, bring it to the attention of the group and have them create targeted norms to resolve it:

- If a distracting side-chat takes place and you feel you need to intervene, try this language to avoid offending side-chatters:

    "I'm concerned that we've lost you to the conversation and are making decisions without you. Your ideas are valuable; we need you back in the conversation."

At the past few meetings, I've noticed a lot of side-chatting. This is distractng and often keeps us from hearing everyone's comments.

What commitments do we all need to make to ensure that this doesn't happen in the future?

What can and should anyone (including me) say if they notice side-chatting?

- If a topic suddenly causes everyone to turn to someone next to them, try a structured partner chat. Ask each person to find a partner, and set a time frame. Ask the pairs to look at the positive as well as the negative side of the topic. Let them have their focused side-chats, then gather up as much of what the partners discussed as they're willing to share. If you anticipate that no one is likely to speak up, call for a break. During it, ask people to write their comments on a flip chart. Review the comments and integrate them into the discussion.

- If specific people are persistent side-chatters, take them aside and offer them feedback:

    "I've noticed that you engaged in several lengthy side-chats at today's meeting. I found this to be very distracting. Would you please stop doing this in future meetings?"

*TIP

When senior people side-chat habitually, your best strategy is talking to them privately rather than in front of their staff.

17 Side-Trackers

"On another note . . ."

The Challenge

- Discussions wander from item to item without closure of previous conversations.
- The agenda is largely ignored or even abandoned.
- Certain individuals in the group have a habit of bringing up extraneous topics.
- People leave the meeting with a sense of frustration from lack of closure.

"Let me take a few minutes to tell you about the meeting I went to last week."

There he goes again!

What's Really Going On

- The group may have a pattern of addressing too many agenda items, which forces them to race from topic to topic.
  - Members may lack effective meeting skills.
  - The group may lack specific, norms about side-tracking.
- If norms do exist, the group may be failing to honor them.
- Some individuals do this to get attention and exert control.
- Side-tracking is sometimes a power play by individuals to refocus the meeting on their pet issues.

Facilitator Pitfalls

- Allowing the side-tracking to continue without checking to see if the topic is one that the group wants to pursue.
- Going along for the ride and facilitating each new side conversation.
- Allowing the group to operate without specific norms to deal with digressions.
- Allowing the group to wander from topic to topic without pointing out the lack of closure on previous topics.
- Silently hoping the group will stop digressing on its own.

I wish they wouldn't constantly digress!

Intervention Strategies

- Provide training on meeting effectiveness.
- Bring side-tracks to the attention of the group as soon as they occur so that members can decide if the new topic should be pursued:

    "I'm noticing that you just moved to a new topic that isn't on the agenda.
    I'm concerned that this is going to take time from other items.
    Is this the topic you want to pursue right now or do you want to park it?"

- Create a "Parking Lot" sheet, and post it on a side wall to record extraneous topics.

"Parking Lot"

- Help the group create targeted norms at the start of the meeting to deal with side-tracking by asking:

    What should we do at today's meeting to ensure that we don't jump from topic to topic?

    What should we do if we notice side-tracking?

    How will we know that we have closure on a topic and that it's ok to move on?

    What constitutes closure?

- Secure more power for yourself by asking:

"What should I say or do if I notice the meeting has gone off track?"

*TIP
Be careful not to let the discussion about whether to end a side-track become a major side-track itself! Always place time limits on process discussions.

18 Blocking
"I simply won't support this decision."

"No way I'm going along with that!"

The Challenge

- Blocking occurs when folks say "yeah-but" as soon as an idea is put forward, even before they hear all the details.
- Someone declares that they will absolutely not support an idea, often just after a final decision has been made.
- Blockers are good at identifying why something won't work, but may not have a lot of ideas to contribute.

What's Really Going On

- Blocking is sometimes an unconscious behavior in habitually negative or cynical individuals.
- Conscious blocking may be a power play by an individual to gain control or to get his or her way.

- Blocking may be an attention-getting tactic by a member who feels excluded or rejected by their group.
- Blockers may be playing a bargaining game in which they eventually agree to support the group's idea in exchange for people endorsing one of their ideas.

Facilitator Pitfalls

- Allowing blocking to derail a meeting without making an intervention.
- Failing to understand that blocking may be a sign of low trust and lack of group cohesion.
- Failing to offer helpful feedback to the chronic blocker.
- Failing to be alert to patterns of blocking, especially in groups that have difficulty coming to closure.

I wonder why these guys can never make a decision?

Intervention Strategies

- Help the group create norms that specifically address blocking *before* it happens by asking:

- If the group fails to set norms to deal with blocking, it may be necessary to offer a set of norms for members to ratify:

> What can we do at today's meeting to ensure that all ideas are given a fair hearing?
>
> If someone wants to oppose an idea, how do we want them to do that?

> To avoid blocking at our meetings we will:
>
> Monitor ourselves to notice if we start to say no to an idea without really hearing the details or giving it a chance to be considered.
>
> Encourage each other to listen and be open to alternative suggestions and new ideas.
>
> Be willing to compromise and accommodate others in order to support the group.

- Offer immediate feedback when blocking takes place using the three-part verbal intervention model:

  "I'm noticing that the past three ideas have been dismissed without much discussion. I'm concerned that you may be missing some good ideas. Please listen carefully to ideas and explore them before discarding them."

- Challenge blockers to substantiate why they're rejecting an idea and to provide the group with alternatives.

- Use a forcefield analysis to engage the blocker in looking at the pros in addition to the cons of an idea.

- Meet one-on-one with blockers to coach them on their behavior.

*TIP
Blockers need to know that you're on to their tactics and that you won't hesitate to deal with them assertively!

19 Unresolved Conflicts
"This goes way back!"

The Challenge

- Throughout the meeting, two or more individuals make emotionally laden comments that don't relate to the current discussion.
- Neither party supports the ideas put forward by the other.
- The parties make sarcastic or snide comments about each other.
- The issue at the heart of the conflict is only alluded to indirectly.
- Other group members may have taken sides, polarizing the group.
- Outside the meeting, the combatants try to build support for their side of the dispute.

"There you go again!"

"You should talk!"

What's Really Going On

- A lingering, unresolved conflict between two or more individuals is being played out in the meeting.
- Trust levels and cohesion within the group are compromised.
- The tensions adversely affect the group's ability to function effectively.
- People may lack the skills needed to resolve sensitive disputes.

Facilitator Pitfalls

- Allowing the unresolved conflict to poison the group atmosphere without taking action to resolve it.
- Meeting privately with one party to hear the concerns, but not with the other.
- Letting any one party think you agree with them.
- Unconsciously taking sides by doing things like letting one party speak more or making more eye contact with one party than the other.
- Forfeiting your neutrality by solving the problem for the parties or by telling them what to do or how to behave.
- Forcing the conflict into the open despite the group's lack of skills and sufficient trust to resolve the conflict.

Intervention Strategies

- Ask a senior person for the authority to conduct a mediation or secure the consent of the parties in conflict.
- If parties are unwilling to meet, inform them that they can no longer air their differences during meetings. State clearly and firmly that their only chance to resolve the dispute confidentially and off the record is by meeting with you.
- Interview each of the parties individually to gain a balanced understanding of the nature of the dispute. Emphasize that you are *not* taking sides.
- Facilitate a private session with the parties, during which you enforce these rules:

1. One person will present their view of the situation.
2. The other person will not speak except to ask clarifying questions. The listener must make notes about the other person's views.
3. When the first person is finished, the second person will give a summary of what he or she heard.
4. If the first person is satisfied that they were heard correctly, the process will be repeated.
5. At no point will anyone interrupt or argue.
6. Everyone will maintain neutral body language.
7. The facilitator can and will stop proceedings if any rule is broken.
8. Once both parties agree that they have been heard, there will be a recess during which each party answers two questions:
   "What I need from you to put this behind us . . . and . . . What I'm offering you in return."
9. The parties reconvene to share their needs and offers and make a commitment to act on them.
10. All conversations will be kept confidential and not be shared with other group members.

- Create a follow-up process for six to eight weeks later, in which each party rates the extent to which the other person kept their commitments.
- Privately offer the parties regular feedback concerning their conduct at meetings.

*TIP
Old festering conflicts are best dealt with off-site, because privacy encourages both openness and a greater willingness to accommodate.

20 Cynicism
"Why bother!"

"This won't work!"

"Nothing's ever going to change!"

"Just another flavor-of-the-month idea!"

The Challenge

- Every idea gets a negative reception.
- People are unwilling to talk about doing things differently.
- People act stressed and distracted during the meeting, citing work pressures as the culprit.
- The group sees hidden agendas and sinister motives behind every activity.

What's Really Going On

- Participants may be cynical because of previous failed or unsupported events.
- People may be feeling overworked and undercompensated.
- People may have developed an "us against them" attitude against upper management.

"Come on you guys! I took you for a bunch of real go-getters!"

Facilitator Pitfalls

- Ignoring the cynical comments and simply forging ahead with the meeting.
- Berating people for being cynical.
- Cajoling members into being more positive.
- Using a jolly, cheerleading approach.

Intervention Strategies

- Check out your perception that cynicism is affecting the group's outlook. Ask members about causes to vent negative feelings:

  "I'd like to check out a sense I'm getting that many of you have a cynical view of things. Am I reading this right? Tell me where this comes from."

- Neutrally record all responses, then ask members which are within their control and which are outside their control.

- Facilitate discussions to identify strategies for the items within the group's control. Then work on strategies to influence the items that are outside the group's control.

Why we're cynical	What can be done
Lack of information from above	Ask for management contact person
Not enough computers for the project	Write up tech needs document

- Engage the group in developing norms to deal with cynicism before it occurs:

- Respond to isolated incidents of cynicism with immediate feedback using the three-part verbal intervention model:

  "I'm noticing that the last two ideas were quickly dismissed. I'm concerned that you may not be giving these proposals a chance. I need you to listen with a more open mind and focus on the pros as well as the cons of each idea."

*TIP

Cynicism can only be overcome by naming it and engaging group members in finding strategies to change the group climate.

What can we do at today's meeting to ensure that we stay positive and open to new ideas?

What should we do if we notice that we're becoming overly negative?

21 Sarcasm
"This is typical of you!"

The Challenge

- Some individuals in the group make negative comments about every proposal.
- Others use a cutting tone whenever they speak.
- You notice negative gestures like shrugging, not making eye contact, and using aggressive hand motions.
- Members respond to each other with negative slurs, put-downs, and innuendos.
- Rather than being direct about concerns, members subtly reveal their anger through their tone of voice or body language.

"Here you go again! Another great idea!"

"I knew we could count on you for support!"

"Now, now; let's all be nice!"

What's Really Going On

- There may be unresolved interpersonal conflicts simmering beneath the surface.
- Sarcastic people are often deeply angry about past disappointments in their personal or work life.
- People may lack interpersonal skills.
- The group may have drifted into a pattern of inappropriate behavior.
- Group members may lack respect and trust for each other.
- The group probably lacks norms to encourage effective behaviors.

Facilitator Pitfalls

- Allowing people to make sarcastic comments without intervening.
- Failing to create a safe environment where unresolved issues can be surfaced.
- Making weak-sounding pleas for cooperation.

Intervention Strategies

- Meet with group members individually outside the meeting to determine if unresolved issues between specific parties may call for private mediation.
- Provide training in effective meeting behaviors.
- Help the group develop targeted norms that discourage sarcasm by asking:

> How should we act to let others know that we respect both them and their ideas?
>
> What commitments can we each make about how we talk to others?
>
> What is it ok for anyone to say if they sense a caustic tone is hurting the atmosphere?

- Make people aware that they're breaking a group norm whenever sarcasm occurs:

"Let's remember the rules you set about using positive language and being respectful."

- Use the intervention language model to redirect sarcasm, saying:

"Sally, I'm concerned that your tone of voice may be getting in the way of people hearing your excellent points. Please start again in a more neutral way."

- Include the issue of sarcasm on an exit survey so that the group can give itself feedback and create new norms to improve interactions.

*TIP

Sarcasm is nearly always a deliberately aggressive tactic that has a corrosive effect on relationships. It always needs to be dealt with as soon as it occurs.

To what extent do we talk to each other in a respectful and positive manner?

1_____2_____3_____4_____5
Never   Sometimes   Always

To what extent does sarcasm creep into the conversational tone?

1_____2_____3_____4_____5
Never   Sometimes   Always

22 Stuck

"Are we still talking about that?"

The Challenge

- The group is stuck on one topic and going in circles.
- Suggestions about closure fall on deaf ears.
- When asked to move on, members insist that they can't and call for more data or more discussion.
- Individuals keep repeating points over and over.
- At the end of the discussion, people are pretty much in the same place they were at the beginning.

"Let's get more data!"

"Let's get more opinions!"

"Let's discuss this some more!"

Facilitator Pitfalls

- Allowing discussions to continue endlessly without setting time limits for closure or for parking unresolved items.
- Failing to recognize participants may use spinning as a deliberate power play or delaying tactic.
- Failing to provide adequate structure for entrenched discussions.
- Allowing individuals to dig deep trenches around their positions so that alternatives become impossible.
- Failing to recognize that some groups have a self-defeating tendency to do endless data collection and/or suffer from analysis/paralysis.

What's Really Going On

- The group really may be missing data.
- Some groups are predisposed to endless data gathering and overanalysis.
- Group members may be stuck in entrenched thinking and unable to see outside the box.
- One or more individuals may be fixated on a solution that they're trying to push on the group.
- There may be a lack of willingness by individuals to compromise for the sake of progress.
- The group may need external input or fresh perspectives.

Intervention Strategies

- Offer the group feedback about their tendency to get stuck and engage them in setting targeted norms that prevent future spinning:

  "At the last meeting, you got stuck on one topic, which made it impossible to move forward or arrive at a decision. To ensure this doesn't happen at today's meeting, let's talk about:"

Why did we get stuck, and what can we do today to avoid these pitfalls?"

What can anybody say or do if discussions get stuck at today's meeting?

- Establish reasonable time limits for each discussion, and ask a group member to act as timekeeper.

- Help the group identify how much data is enough, and encourage members to do their homework.

- Offer training about various decision-making tools. Decide which decisions need to be made using consensus, which ought to be delegated to individuals, and which to make by voting.

- If members are stuck in traditional thinking, introduce key steps from a creative problem-solving model to encourage members to think outside the box.

- If the group needs fresh ideas, encourage people to go outside the group to gather input or suggest inviting outsiders for specific discussions.

- If the topic keeps getting wider, introduce a process tool, like a "Criteria-Based Decision Grid" or "Multivoting" to help narrow the focus.

- If people are stuck in polarized positions, restructure the discussions. Begin with the current situation or need and then use "Brainstorming" and a "Criteria-Based Decision Grid" to generate a consensus decision.

- Offer clear feedback each time the conversation gets stuck and engage members in identifying improvement strategies:

  "I notice you've been on this topic a while without making progress. What can we do to get unstuck?"

*TIP

If a group has a tendency to get bogged down, engage them in developing strategies to move forward.

23 Conflict Erupts
"Let me tell you how I really feel!"

The Challenge

- Tensions that have been simmering suddenly boil over.
- Conversations get personal.
- People become emotional, talk over each other, and raise their voices.
- Other members withdraw in uncomfortable silence.
- Focus is lost and relationships are damaged.

What's Really Going On

- There may be an old suppressed issue.
- Group members may lack conflict management skills.
- The group may lack a system for safely giving and receiving feedback.
- Group norms, if they exist at all, are being ignored.
- Focus and objectivity are lost as people speak from an emotional perspective.
- Group cohesion is destroyed as people take sides or completely withdraw.
- The future ability of the group to function is jeopardized.

Facilitator Pitfalls

- Retreating to the sidelines while group members fight.
- Failing to bring structure to conflicts.
- Assuming that calling for a break will solve the problem.
- Not establishing clear rules and boundaries for sensitive discussions.
- Not checking with the whole group about whether the conflict should be addressed inside or outside the meeting.
- Making weak-sounding statements when asking members to stop fighting.

Intervention Strategies

- Adopt a firm, calm demeanor.
- Point out which behaviors are acceptable and which are not.
- Ask questions about the nature of the conflict to determine whether it's resolvable or whether it should be addressed in private.
- If a conflict does get played out in front of others, impose rules:

    "If we're going to have disagreements, I'm going to insist that only one person talk at a time. When one speaker has finished, the next person must give a short summary of that speaker's views before sharing his or her opposing views."

- Throughout all exchanges, facilitate very assertively, never hesitating to stop people, even in mid-sentence, if their behaviors become inappropriate:

    "I'm going to stop you and ask you to start over; this time, please make your points in a more neutral way."

- If arguing is an ongoing pattern in the group, help members establish targeted norms by asking:

    "Arguing can result in damaged relationships. How can we share differences of opinion so that this doesn't happen? What rules do we need to put into place? How should people speak to each other? What other guidelines will make us more effective in dealing with our differences?"

- Provide structure by using a tool such as "Forcefield Analysis" or a "Criteria-Based Decision Grid" to bring more objectivity to heated discussions.
- If unresolved interpersonal issues continue to cause conflict, implement a peer feedback process so that members can safely vent concerns and offer each other improvement suggestions.

*TIP
Group conflicts demand that you remain totally neutral, yet act very assertively to ensure that rules are created and followed.

What you do that's effective . . .

What you could do to be more effective . . .

24 A Member Storms Out
"I'm not listening to this!"

The Challenge

- The meeting seems to be going fine when one person suddenly gets up and walks out.
- He or she may or may not say anything as they leave.
- The remaining group members look bewildered and upset.
- The meeting screeches to a halt as a heavy feeling settles over the room.

What's Really Going On

- The conversation may have touched on an unresolved issue or sensitive topic.
- One or more group members may have said something that was inappropriate or insulting.
- A comment may have been misunderstood.
- The person who walked out may feel unsupported by the group or the group's leader.
- This person may have serious personal or emotional problems.
- The walk-out may have been a staged drama that's part of a larger dispute between the individual and the organization.

Facilitator Pitfalls

- Failing to assess the history of the group, including the existence of unresolved issues.
- Underestimating how sensitive a topic might be to certain individuals.
- Failing to create safety norms for potentially sensitive conversations.
- Making the assumption that there's sufficient trust and cohesion in the group to discuss sensitive topics openly.
- Not discriminating between the types of disputes a facilitator can resolve and those that fall outside any facilitator's domain.
- Sweeping the issue under the rug rather than letting the group vent productively and move forward.

"Too bad she left. Oh well; we have a lot to get done so we'd better get to it!"

Intervention Strategies

- Conduct pre-meeting interviews to uncover sensitive or unresolved issues.
- Preview the agenda and design with the leader and group members to check for sensitivities.
- If there's a difficult conversation that can't be avoided, discuss the norming questions below with participants in pre-meeting interviews:

- Or use these same questions to start any meeting that could become sensitive. This targeted norming discussion will establish a safe climate for the meeting:

- If someone does walk out, acknowledge it and let people vent. Steer people away from making negative comments about the person:

"I'm noticing that some people look upset, so let's talk about what just happened and what we can do to get this person back."

We have an issue on the agenda that some individuals may find difficult to discuss.

What conditions or assurances do people need to feel comfortable enough to do this?

What other rules do we need to abide by throughout this discussion?

If anyone ever feels uncomfortable or personally attacked, what is ok for them to say or do?

- If a group member insulted the departed teammate, it's his or her responsibility to apologize to the person for the inappropriate remark.

- During a break or after the meeting, contact the individual who walked out and acknowledge the difficulty of the situation. Communicate that the group would like him or her to return, and ask under what conditions the individual would consider returning. Help negotiate his or her return to the group.

*TIP
Be realistic about which problems the group can deal with and which are too sensitive.

25 Unwilling to Take Responsibility

"I'm not doing it!"

"I don't have the skills!"   "I'm too busy!"   "I don't get paid for this!"

The Challenge

- As soon as the group identifies action plans, people start making excuses about why they can't take responsibility.
- The reliable workhorses volunteer while others evade responsibility.
- Members start to give assignments to individuals who aren't at the meeting.
- Some group members insist that you take on the action items.

What's Really Going On

- Some individuals may lack skills necessary to take on tasks.
- Others may be feeling that they're already overworked.
- There may not be a mechanism to reward or recognize extra effort.
- The group may be lacking cohesion; people don't feel any sense of responsibility for each other.
- People may be wary if a past assignment didn't get organizational support or yield results.
- Evading responsibility may be a deliberate ploy by people who are harboring a personal grudge.

Facilitator Pitfalls

- Allowing people to assign work to absent individuals.
- Loading more work on the same few people who always volunteer.
- Not surfacing or dealing with resistance to taking responsibility.
- Letting people leave the meeting without next steps.
- Allowing the group to foist assignments on you.

"Ok, I'll do it!"

Intervention Strategies

- Tell people to expect follow-on activities right at the start of the project or meeting.
- Help the group create a targeted norm about members taking responsibility for implementation activities:

- Engage members in a problem-solving conversation about what's keeping them from taking on assignments.

- Conduct a skills needs assessment and arrange for specific training to help people overcome skills barriers.

- Create coaching relationships so that experienced people are available to provide support to inexperienced team members.

- Seek outside assistance to remove the systemic blocks that people feel are discouraging them, and, where possible, get senior managers to act as champions for assignments.

- State clearly that it's not your role to take responsibility for action items:

- Implement project-planning processes like "Gannt Charts" to help members track projects and add a measure of accountability.

- Put a "Bring Forward" item on future agendas to ensure the group reviews past work and that people feel recognized for their efforts.

All of your good work today is going to be wasted if we don't follow up.

What commitments are you prepared to make today to ensure that this project moves forward?

How can we ensure that work gets divided evenly and doesn't all fall on a few people?

"You need to know that I will _not_ be doing the follow-up work on this project."

*TIP
Identifying blocks, removing organizational barriers, and ensuring personal accountability are critical intervention strategies.

26 Losing Authority
"Have I lost you?"

The Challenge

- Group members who had been following your process suggestions and actively participating are now quiet and questioning your approach.
- The process you've selected isn't yielding results, and the conversation seems to be stuck.
- People shift restlessly, and you detect growing frustration with your performance.
- Someone suggests a change in facilitators.

What's Really Going On

- You may have lost the confidence of the group.
- You may not have the skills or experience to deal with the matter under discussion.
- You may be operating under incorrect assumptions about the situation.
- You may not have done enough homework to be able to ask the right questions or identify effective process tools.
- You may be moving at the wrong pace.
- You may have lost the respect of the group by not being able to deal with ineffective behaviors.

Facilitator Pitfalls

- Not checking key assumptions at the start of the session.
- Ignoring the signs that you've lost the group and simply carrying on.
- Calling for a break in the hope that a rest will fix the problem.
- Failing to stop the process to get feedback about its effectiveness.
- Waiting until the meeting is over to check with participants about whether you had lost their confidence.

- You may have unintentionally lost your neutrality by changing people's words when recording ideas or by appearing to favor one idea over another.
- You may have inadvertently slipped out of the neutral role and begun to take part in the content of the discussions.

"I sense I lost everbody about two hours ago!"

Intervention Strategies

- Prepare sufficiently to understand the desired outcomes of the session, the dynamics of the group, and any special challenges.
- Create a detailed agenda that includes alternative approaches in case specific tools don't work.
- Clearly state the operating assumptions at the beginning of the session to test their accuracy, i.e., the goal of the session, expected outcomes, constraints, time frames, key stakeholders, the decision-making authority of the group, etc.
- Periodically take the group's pulse to get feedback on how things are going:

  "I want to check with you. How's the pace? Is this process working? Are we making progress? Are you still with me or have I lost you?"

- If you sense you may have lost the confidence of the group, courageously ask for feedback and guidance:

  "I sense I've lost you. What can I do to regain your confidence?"

Midpoint Check

To what extent are we making progress?

1 _____ 2 _____ 3 _____ 4 _____ 5
None   Some   A lot

Rate the quality of our ideas and decisions.

1 _____ 2 _____ 3 _____ 4 _____ 5
Poor   Fair   Satisfactory   Good   Excellent

Is the process or approach we're using working?

1 _____ 2 _____ 3 _____ 4 _____ 5
Not at all   Not sure   Absolutely

How much confidence do you have in the facilitator?

1 _____ 2 _____ 3 _____ 4 _____ 5
Poor   Fair   Satisfactory   Good   Excellent

- Provide an anonymous mid-point check so people can express concerns.

- Stay out of the room while a volunteer facilitator helps the group debrief the survey and identify improvement ideas, including suggestions for you.

- If you regularly experience loss of "followership," ask an experienced facilitator to observe your work and offer you feedback.

*TIP
Experienced facilitators are always alert for signs they've lost the group and immediately take steps to regain participant confidence.

27 Blocked Consensus
"Why can't we agree?"

The Challenge

- After lengthy deliberations, group members can't reach a decision.
- Sometimes just one person is holding out; at other times the impasse represents a split in the group.
- Frustration and anger set in as members try to convince or even bully colleagues into going along with the group opinion.
- Just to end the impasse, some members give in, then distance themselves from the outcome as soon as the meeting's over.

"I never really supported that idea!"

"Me neither!"

What's Really Going On

- The group may be unclear about the nature of consensus and may lack group decision-making skills.
- Member unwillingness to accommodate may indicate low trust levels.
- One or more members may be blocking a decision for personal reasons.
- Group members may have become locked into positional thinking early in the discussion and are unable to see alternatives.
- The decision-making process may be faulty or based on insufficient data.

Facilitator Pitfalls

- Failing to clarify the meaning of consensus or provide needed skills.
- Allowing a group to operate without adequate norms to guide them through difficult decision-making sessions.
- Allowing a group to remain deadlocked for extended periods of time.
- Sticking with a process that isn't yielding results.
- Failing to be inclusive and careful about wording while crafting a consensus statement.
- Not making assertive verbal interventions to redirect inappropriate behaviors.
- Failing to test group member commitment to the final decision.

Intervention Strategies

- Set appropriate time frames for all decision processes.
- If a group becomes stuck, stop the discussion and assess why it's happening.
- Reexamine the process and be ready to offer an alternative tool or technique.
- If positional thinking is blocking consensus, shift the process to one of joint analysis and brainstorming.
- Help the group set norms that will establish positive decision-making behaviors by asking targeted norming questions:

> How can we ensure that we stay open to others' ideas and not get stuck on a predetermined solution?
>
> What frame of mind do we each need to adopt to meet each other halfway?

- To encourage people to become more accommodating, clarify that consensus means that people can live with the outcome and not that everyone totally agrees with the outcome.
- When the group is unable to all buy in to a consensus statement, draw a "Gradients of Agreement" scale on a flip chart. Point out that 4 is the point of consensus, not 5. Describe each point on the chart, and ask people to identify where they think they are relative to the consensus statement:

1	2	3	4	5
I'm totally opposed and have philosophical differences with the solutions	I have several serious reservations about the proposed solution	I have one or two reservations about the proposed solution	I can live with the proposed solution	I'm in total agreement with the proposed solution

- Invite those who placed themselves at 1, 2 or 3 to indicate why. Ask them what amendments to the consensus statement would move them toward 4. Explore the possibility of adding these amendments to the consensus statement.
- Once a consensus has been reached, get a public commitment from each person by asking them if they will support the decision.

> *TIP
> If the group has a pattern of difficulties reaching consensus, they may need to set aside time to do some focused problem solving on why they become deadlocked.

28 Lack of Closure

"Let's finish this later."

The Challenge

- After lengthy discussion, the conversation is suddenly terminated without closure.
- The conversation keeps drifting from topic to topic.
- Topics get sent to the "Parking Lot" as soon as they become difficult or complex.
- No one in the group attempts to summarize conversations or identify next steps.
- Group members resist your suggestion that they appoint a minute taker and balk at recording the proceedings.
- The same topics are dealt with at meeting after meeting.

What's Really Going On

- Group members may not be doing their homework and may lack the data they need to make decisions.
- The organization may be unwilling to grant the group the decision-making power it needs to actually make decisions.
- The group may need training in the dynamics of effective meetings.
- Group members may lack clear norms for managing their conversations.
- People may be delaying to avoid more work.
- The group may be in this dysfunctional pattern from years of poorly structured and badly led meetings.
- The members may deliberately want to avoid change.

Facilitator Pitfalls

- Failing to stop group members from flowing from one topic to the next.
- Failing to insist on closure.
- Lacking a method for bringing closure to discussions.
- Failing to retrieve items sent to the "Parking Lot."
- Failing to insist that the group address unfinished business.
- Neglecting to offer feedback to the group about its lack of closure.

"Let's leave this item for now and deal with it at the next meeting."

Intervention Strategies

- Clarify whether the group has sufficient power to make decisions.
- Determine if people have sufficient information and if the right people are present.
- Set time frames around each discussion and appoint a timekeeper.
- Specify expected results at the start of each discussion so that members are clear about the intent of each conversation:

  "Let's get clear about the expected outcome at the start of this discussion. Are you sharing information, offering advice, making recommendations or trying to arrive at a final decision? Does this conversation need to end in action steps?"

- Help the group create norms to address lack of closure. These norming questions might read:

How do we ensure that we have closure on each topic before moving forward?

Under what conditions is it acceptable to park or delay an item?

- Offer the group frequent summaries, both verbally and in writing, to help them arrive at timely conclusions:

  "Let me review what you've said to see if this sounds like a conclusion."

- Enroll participants in inventing a non-threatening phrase when they notice a digression:

"We're skipping again!"

- If the group persists in jumping from topic to topic without closure, set aside time at a future meeting to problem solve the issue of lack of closure.

*TIP
Not achieving closure is often a sign that a group lacks clear parameters and accountability.

29 Lack of Feedback
"Let's talk later!"

The Challenge

- No one speaks up when asked for an opinion about sensitive or difficult subjects.
- People's body language indicates that they aren't expressing their concerns.
- A few people do all of the talking while others sit in silence.
- Decisions are made without thorough analysis and discussion.
- People go along with decisions without saying what's on their mind.

"I'm not saying anything!"

"Me neither!"

What's Really Going On

- Trust levels may be so low that only a few outspoken people feel they can say what's on their mind.
- There may be a history of retaliation for expressing negative or contrary viewpoints.
- The culture of the organization probably isn't used to giving and receiving feedback.
- The group may have a pattern of avoiding sensitive issues.
- The organization may have a top-down environment in which leaders are unaccustomed to employee participation.

Facilitator Pitfalls

- Failing to research the history and culture of the organization.
- Ignoring the suppressed looks and withdrawn body language.
- Leaving the quiet people out of the discussion.
- Letting the group make important decisions without input from everyone.
- Failing to provide feedback mechanisms for surfacing issues and concerns.

No one's saying anything, so I guess everything's ok?

Intervention Strategies

- Conduct one-on-one interviews with group members to gain an understanding of why people might be holding back.
- Conduct a climate survey to generate data regarding trust and openness levels.
- Meet with the leader to share concerns about the lack of feedback and get his or her agreement to use participative strategies.
- Use a variety of approaches that encourage participation, such as small groups, asking people to interview a partner, and having people write comments on flip charts or on small slips of paper.
- Help the group complete a "Resistance Chart" and ask them what it would take to move forward:

    1) Ask people to secretly rate where they are on a scale of 1 to 5:

1	2	3	4	5
I don't feel free to speak out		I sometimes feel I can speak freely		I feel I can say anything at any time

    2) Ask people to identify what assurances or conditions would encourage them to shift their rating to the right on the scale. Record their comments. These will be either new norms or action plans.

- Conduct "Exit Surveys" to ensure that negative feelings have a productive outlet. Bring forward the survey at the start of the next meeting, and facilitate a discussion of what would improve each rating. Implement suggestions immediately.

*TIP

Without feedback, problems repeat themselves and circulate on the rumor mill.

Exit Survey

At today's meeting, to what extent:

Did we make good use of our time?

1_____2_____3_____4_____5

Did we make quality decisions?

1_____2_____3_____4_____5

Were you able to speak your mind freely?

1_____2_____3_____4_____5

Were your views taken into account?

1_____2_____3_____4_____5

30 Lack of Follow-Through

"Nothing ever happens!"

The Challenge

- People work hard to create strategies and action plans but nothing gets implemented.
- People hold back because of past failures.
- Constantly shifting priorities leave people wary of investing themselves in new inititatives.

"I'm not getting involved this time!!"

"What happened to the last batch of recommendations?"

"We did all this before!"

What's Really Going On

- People may be justifiably resistant toward new projects or activities that revisit territory already covered in past efforts.
- Management may be going through the motions on specific initiatives just to say they were addressed, with no real intent to follow through.
- Past projects may have been established without sufficient resources or organizational supports.
- People may feel overworked and reluctant to take on additional assignments.

"Please be positive. It's all going to be different this time!"

Facilitator Pitfalls

- Failing to explore the past history of the group with similar assignments.
- Ignoring group member feelings and concerns.
- Relying on having a senior management representative present to coerce people to take part.
- Selling people on the notion that this time the process will be different.
- Encouraging the group to forge ahead without addressing the reasons for past failures.

Intervention Strategies

- Conduct one-on-one interviews before any major new inititiave to find out what happened to past projects.

- Meet with senior managers to gain their cooperation as champions for the recommendations made by the group.

- Take a problem-solving approach to the issue of poor follow-through by engaging members in analyzing the situation and brainstorming ideas to ensure that action items are implemented:

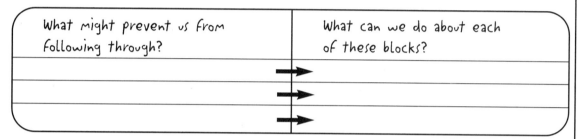

What might prevent us from following through?	What can we do about each of these blocks?

- Allocate sufficient time at the end of each agenda item for action planning, then test those plans to make sure they're realistic. Anticipate blocks and barriers to each.

- Always ensure that there are specific measurable objectives for each action item so people are clear about their roles and responsibilities.

- Help the group create a planning chart to track next steps and ensure proper management of follow-through.

- Create a "Bring Forward" segment at all meetings so members know that they will be accountable to report on progress.

- Keep senior managers in the loop by periodically inviting them to meetings to hear progress reports and to provide support.

- Link project accountabilities to performance appraisals so that members feel committed to taking action.

- Celebrate successes to give the group a sense of achievement.

*TIP
Lack of follow-through is a major source of cynicism and needs attention.

Notes

4
Consulting Strategies for Facilitators

EXCEPT FOR REGULAR STAFF MEETINGS AND THOSE SMALL, impromptu facilitations that we're all asked to do from time to time, facilitation assignments are best positioned within a defined series of steps.

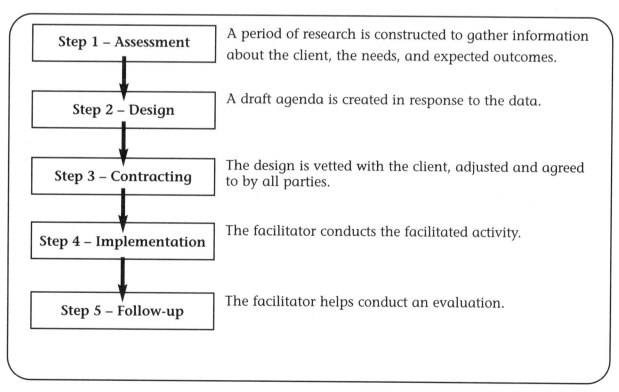

Step 1 – Assessment	A period of research is constructed to gather information about the client, the needs, and expected outcomes.
Step 2 – Design	A draft agenda is created in response to the data.
Step 3 – Contracting	The design is vetted with the client, adjusted and agreed to by all parties.
Step 4 – Implementation	The facilitator conducts the facilitated activity.
Step 5 – Follow-up	The facilitator helps conduct an evaluation.

These steps are similar to the steps that consultants use to manage their work. As you advance from simple facilitations to more complex assignments, it's a wise strategy to borrow this approach from the world of consulting. When you use these steps, you'll discover that it gives your work boundaries and helps guard against hastily created activities that later prove to be ineffective or lack client buy-in.

When an external facilitator follows these steps, it helps create clear parameters for the scope of the work to be completed. When an internal facilitator deploys them, it helps them to define the boundaries of their work and negotiate the power and support they need in order to be effective.

You will notice that the terms consultant and client are used throughout this section of the book. In fact, the term facilitator is often used interchangeably with the term consultant. This overlap is due to the large number of traits they have in common.

Consulting is:

- a contracted, short-term assignment; often part-time
- a role specifically designed to meet the needs of the assignment
- conducted in another organization or another part of your organization where you're an outsider
- an assignment in which you have no direct authority over the people or programs involved
- a role in which power stems from technical expertise, interpersonal style, and process skills
- a role where the main contribution, besides providing those skills, is to help clients understand the real nature of their problem
- a role in which you report to the person or persons who are being helped, rather than to the hierarchical head of the organization
- a role that has a defined end date at which time your connection to the assignment and the people involved terminates.

One of the key strategies that will help you to be both more effective and to be taken more seriously is to conduct all of your facilitation assignments as a consultant. You can do this by following the five-step model described in the following pages as your roadmap.

Applying the Five Steps

These steps can be applied to virtually all facilitation assignments ranging from a one-day problem-solving meeting to a lengthy change management project. The length of time required to complete each step will depend, of course, on the scale of the facilitation assignment.

It's important to note that these steps are relevant even when there is little or no time for pre-work. Below is an example of how these steps might look if they were to be incorporated right into an agenda for which the facilitator had no time to prepare:

Welcome and Warm-up	Opening comments and welcome. Team energizer.
Objectives Overview	Review of the stated objectives for the meeting.
Needs Assessment	Use of Sequential Questioning, Open Space, or an Entrance Survey to identify key issues and needs.
Survey Feedback	Report back and interpretation of data by participants. Identification of expected outcomes.
Agenda Ratification and Contracting	Facilitator's process proposal and acceptance by participants.
Facilitated Dialogue	Implementation of the ratified design.
Facilitated Dialogue	Process continues.
Summary and Closure	Review of agreements and next steps planning.
Evaluation	Exit Survey to assess degree to which expected results were achieved.

Advanced facilitators utilize the steps in the facilitation process regardless of the length of an assignment as a strategy that gives their work structure and adds an aura of professionalism.

Step 1 - Assessment

Thoroughly assessing the client's situation is the critical first step in designing and leading any effective meeting, whether that meeting is a stand-alone event or part of a series of conversations within a larger process.

Facilitators should try to resist the temptation to plunge into ad hoc sessions or hastily create designs when only a few details have been shared. That's because there can be hidden motives, past conflicts, and other stumbling blocks lurking beneath the surface of even the most innocent-sounding request. Neglecting to do a thorough assessment sets the stage for creating a poor design and misjudging the critical aspects of an assignment.

How This Step Typically Unfolds:

- The facilitator receives a request for assistance. During the initial contact, which is often by telephone, the facilitator asks broad questions to gain a basic understanding of the assignment and makes preliminary notes.
- A face-to-face meeting is held with the person requesting assistance to uncover more information and assess the scope of the assignment.
- If the facilitator judges that he or she is a good match for the assignment, a set of assessment questions is prepared.
- Assessment activities are designed and implemented.

Purpose of This Step:

- to gather important information about the organization, the parties, and the scope of the facilitated activity
- to uncover past history that may exert an impact on discussions
- to assess commitment levels, barriers, resources, resistance factors, and other important circumstances
- to get to know the parties on a one-to-one basis in order to encourage candor and to build rapport
- to identify who the client is
- to determine needed pre-work
- to find out who needs to take part in various discussions

Activities Can Include:

- researching background materials to learn about the client and their work
- identifying key questions and conducting one-on-one interviews with participants
- holding focus groups
- conducting surveys and leading survey-feedback activities

- interviewing stakeholders who may not participate but who play an important role in the process
- analyzing data to create a base for a proposed process design

Challenges of This Step:

- gathering the right background information about the situation
- designing appropriate surveys and asking the right questions
- gaining support for the interviews and surveys
- safely helping client reveal sensitive issues, barriers, and hidden agendas
- establishing rapport with the participants
- communicating important information clearly
- making an accurate diagnosis of the situation and creating a process design that addresses the critical issues

What Can Go Wrong:

- failing to fully understand the culture, needs, and expectations of the participants and their organization
- jumping to conclusions after gathering only preliminary information
- making assumptions about the client and failing to test them
- failing to identify resistance factors and other blocks
- underestimating or intentionally ignoring potential blocks and barriers rather than dealing with them in a forthright manner
- failing to secure the stakeholders needed to provide important support
- communicating unclear or incomplete information

Reasons to Leave the Facilitation Assignment at This Stage*:

- The timeframe does not fit your schedule.
- The assignment requires skills you don't have.
- After analyzing the data it appears clear that the chances for success are poor.
- The resources and other organization supports are not in place.
- There is insufficient openness and trust to address root causes.
- The initiative is mere "window-dressing" and lacks serious intent.

*This is the easiest point to leave a facilitation. Since exiting at later stages becomes increasingly more difficult, it's important to leave early if one or more of the above circumstances are present. If possible inform the client why you're declining the work and leave them with a clear understanding of the type of assignments or situations you might be suited for in the future.

Question Development

A helpful technique for identifying the most effective questions for a specific situation is an exercise borrowed from Peter Block's *Flawless Consulting.* This involves identifying what he refers to as the known and hidden factors. Do this exercise after doing some reading and holding the first preliminary conversations with stakeholders.

Once you've identified your information gaps, develop a set of complex, high-quality questions for use in interviews, surveys, and focus groups.

Known Factors: What have you been told about the situation? What else have you learned so far?

Hidden Factors: What have you not been told? These might be the deeper, more sensitive issues, often the real situation or underlying causes of blocks. What is still unknown to you? What do you need to learn about the organization, the players, the history of past negotiations, etc.?

Sample Assessment Questions

Each facilitation assignment is unique and requires custom-designed questions. These questions can be used to construct a survey or to form the basis of either focus groups or one-on-one interviews. The following are offered simply as examples of questions to consider when planning personal interviews.

You will note that some of the questions assume a level of candor that may not be suitable in all environments. You may even feel that some of the questions are rather risky. These are deliberately included because it's important to look below the surface of a request at this early stage. There may be hidden factors that undermine the potential for success. There may be reasons for you to decline the assignment. It's always far better to ask slightly confrontational questions so that sensitive issues can be surfaced in the relative safety of a private meeting, rather than in the middle of a group gathering.

For examples of specific questions that relate to various interventions, see the Surveys and Evaluations section on the CD-ROM.

- *What's your understanding of this initiative? Do you feel that this activity is needed at this time?*

- *What history should I be aware of? What past events are likely to exert an influence on this activity?*

- *If this initiative were to be totally successful, what would be the best possible outcome?*

- *On a scale of 1 to 5, what do you feel are the chances that this initiative will succeed?*

1	2	3	4	5
no chance		some chance		excellent chance

- *What are some of the positive factors that will help it to succeed?*

- *What are some of the challenges or barriers to success? What's the greatest stumbling block or potential derailer?*

- *Describe the level of openness and trust within this group. Are there likely to be suppressed feelings or hidden conflicts that will operate beneath the surface to exert an influence on proceedings?*

- *Is this a group or a team? Describe one past success of this group. Describe a past failure.*

- *If you could change one parameter or condition surrounding this initiative, what would you change?*

- *How do you personally feel about taking part? What excites you? What worries you?*

- *How would you rate the overall level of commitment of the organization to supporting this initiative? Why?*

1	2	3	4	5
no chance		some chance		excellent chance

- *What resources do you add to this activity?*

- *What's your understanding of my role? What's the best thing that I can contribute? What's the biggest mistake I could make? What advice do you have for me?*

Checklist for Conducting Effective Interviews

One-on-one interviews are one of the best ways to uncover the underlying details of any situation. Private interviews also let you break the ice with group members and build personal connections to individuals.

Since facilitations often feature sensitive aspects, it's important to establish an open and trusting atmosphere. This can be done by explaining that all comments will be kept confidential and that any notes you might make are solely for your planning purposes and will not be shared with any other person.

Whenever the assessment stage calls for interviews, here are some helpful guidelines:

- Find a private place for the interviews.

- Be friendly and take time for informal chatter to establish rapport.

- State your confidentiality guidelines to encourage openness and trust.

- Clearly state the purpose of the interview.

- State only the overall purpose of the initiative before inviting the interviewee to explain their understanding of the initiative.

- Listen more than you talk and paraphrase key points to demonstrate that you are really hearing their points.

- Don't judge, evaluate or reach hasty conclusions.

- Ask follow-on questions that probe to uncover underlying information.

- Ask questions that invite the client to reveal feelings about the process.

- Clarify and validate client feelings. If appropriate, show empathy.

- Clarify what the interviewee wants and needs from the process.

- Remain patient and focused on the client throughout the interview.

- Offer the interviewee a summary of your understanding of their points.

- Check to see if the client is satisfied with both the interview and your understanding of their comments.

- Reiterate how you will be using the information that the interviewee shared.

Identifying the Client

In any consulting project, the person whose needs are being met is referred to as the *client*. It may seem obvious that whoever contacts you to conduct a facilitation assignment automatically becomes your client. It's important to note, however, that in most facilitation activities the client is not the person who makes the initial request for service.

One can take the example of a leader's request that you facilitate a team-building session in his or her department. In this instance, the client is not the leader, but the entire team. The reason the entire team is the client stems from the fact that all of the members will be engaged in making decisions that will not only affect their department, but also will have direct impact on their work lives.

There are instances where the person who requests your assistance is the client. For example, you may be asked to conduct a series of focus groups for a manager who needs the information to include in a report. If the people attending the focus group are not making decisions that will affect them, and if the outcome relates solely to the person requesting your assistance, then that person is indeed your client.

> **Never assume you know
> who the client is – check!**

This is a very important point that must be made crystal clear during the first stage of any facilitation activity. If this isn't clear, you may encounter situations in which:

- the people who contacted you assume you work for them and expect you to do their bidding
- the other participants in the process see you as the agent of the person who contacted you and don't see you as neutral

For these reasons, it's vitally important to always identify who the client is during this first step in the process. To identify who you're working for, ask yourself:

> - Who's directly affected?
> - Whose outcomes are being met?
> - Who needs to trust that I'm working for them?

If you identify that the client for an intervention is the whole group, it's vitally important that you communicate that clearly to the person who's asking for your assistance. Conversely, if you're leading a series of meetings on behalf of a specific person or group, you will need to communicate that to anyone who attends any meeting that's part of the overall initiative.

When you openly state who you're working for and how you conduct your work, it creates trust and helps ensure that your work remains ethical.

Data Analysis Worksheet

The last activity in Step 1 is the creation of a concise data summary to help you with the design stage. This summary is always a confidential document that is not shared with the client. If the process calls for data feedback, a separate document should be prepared that protects the anonymity of respondents.

1) What were you initially told about the nature and purpose of the assignment?

2) What does your data collection indicate to be the actual nature and purpose of the activity? (If there's a change, indicate why this has occurred.)

3) Who is the client? Reasons?

4) What are the important *needs* and *wants* of this initiative? (Rank each list.)

5) What do you now consider to be the expected outcomes? (List in rank order.)

6) Identify the factors at work in this situation:

Things that could help	Things that might hinder

7) What do *you* think are the chances for success? Why?

1	2	3	4	5
no chance		some chance		excellent chance

8) What is the current level of organizational support for this initiative?

1	2	3	4	5
no support		some support		excellent support

9) Who are the key stakeholders? What role does each need to play?

Step 2 - Design

Meetings are complex activities that always need to be carefully designed. This is especially true when a meeting is part of a change initiative. Remember that professional facilitators typically spend a minimum of one hour preparing for every hour spent in front of a group. An experienced facilitator would never venture into a meeting without a detailed design in hand!

The design phase is a time for putting the data from the first step to work. Experienced facilitators typically create several different design options before deciding on the one to use. By considering different approaches, facilitators build in options and flexibility in case the initial approach proves to be ineffective.

How This Step Typically Unfolds:

- The facilitator reviews data collected from site visits, background reading, interviews, surveys, focus groups and process observation, and prepares a data summary.
- If the data-feedback is part of the contracting phase, a separate data summary is written for the client's use.
- The facilitator identifies key meeting elements using the design worksheet and prepares a final draft for review by the client.

Purpose of This Step:

- to interpret the data collected in the assessment step
- to identify the goal, objectives, and expected outcomes
- to identify the activities and process tools needed
- to create a draft meeting design

Activities Can Include:

- reviewing the data and summarizing the findings
- writing a feedback report for the client
- researching related process designs
- creating a written draft design

Challenges of This Step:

- making an accurate assessment of the data
- identifying the appropriate goal, objectives, and outcomes
- identifying effective process elements
- correctly sequencing the activities

What Can Go Wrong:

- hasty, inadequate data review
- underestimating the blocks and barriers
- deliberately ignoring difficult aspects
- failing to build in activities to overcome blocks
- planning activities that are inappropriate to the group
- not planning a number of alternative activities in case an element in the original design proves to be ineffective

Reasons to Leave the Facilitation Assignment at This Stage:*

- The nature of the assignment is inappropriate to a facilitation intervention.
- You have too little experience to be effective in handling this assignment.
- The timeframe set for the activity is totally unrealistic.
- The players identified for the activity are not the ones who need to be involved.
- There's a vast gap between what's wanted and what's needed.
- There are other things such as interpersonal conflicts and trust issues that must be resolved before this activity can succeed.
- No one has the same view of the situation.
- The resources and other organizational supports that are important to the ultimate success of the activity are not present.
- You sense that the activity is a "window dressing" exercise and that there is no sincere intention by the key stakeholders to adhere to the decisions through the facilitated process.

*You may decide to proceed to the next step even if some of the above reasons are in place, but you'll need to negotiate around major barriers. In many assignments, additional sessions are required to deal with one or more such issues before the stage is set to proceed with the original assignment.

Session Design Worksheet

Use the following series of questions to help you begin the design process. Wherever asterisks* appear, jot down the specific process tool or tools to be used for that agenda item.

1) What's the overall goal of the facilitation activity?

_____

2) What are the objectives and expected outcomes of the session?

Objectives   **Expected Outcomes**

i.

_____   ➡️   _____

ii

_____   ➡️   _____

iii

_____   ➡️   _____

iv

_____   ➡️   _____

v

_____   ➡️   _____

3) What's the nature of the conversations that need to be part of this meeting? Assign a percentage to each of the following:

___ % of the meeting that will be information-sharing sessions
___ % of the meeting that will be planning-activities
___ % of the meeting that will be problem-solving activities
___ % of the meeting that will be relationship-building conversations

4) What are the actual decisions that need to be made? How difficult is each decision? What level of empowerment is appropriate for each decision item?

Decisions that need to be made	Difficulty level (1=low, 5=high)	Empowerment level (I, II, III, IV)
*		
*		
*		
*		

5) Who *must* attend?

_____

6) What homework do participants need to do in advance?

_____

7) Does the group need a warm-up exercise to build familiarity or break the ice? If so, what should be its purpose and length?

_____

8) Is there likely to be resistance? If so, what buy-in question or targeted norming question should be asked to overcome that resistance?

_____

9) What else might go wrong during the facilitation? What anticipatory strategies do you need to prepare?

_____

10) What will you say to clarify your role? Who else needs to have their role clarified?

_____

11) What targeted norming questions will you ask in order to create any additional norms that are needed for this session?

_____

12) What power and authority do you need to negotiate in order to be effective before the session? . . . at the start of the session?

_____

13) What questions will you ask during a midpoint check? . . . at the end of the session?

_____

Session Design Components

All meetings are made up of a complex combination of several of the following types of activities:

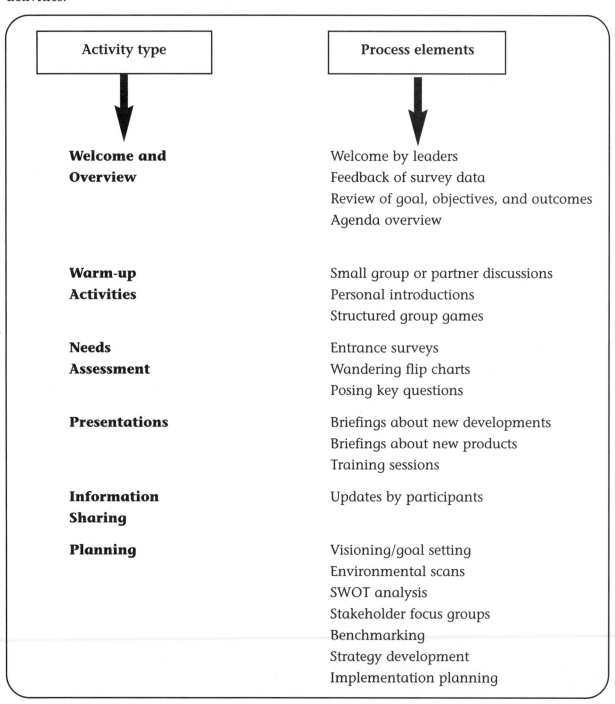

Activity type	Process elements
Welcome and Overview	Welcome by leaders Feedback of survey data Review of goal, objectives, and outcomes Agenda overview
Warm-up Activities	Small group or partner discussions Personal introductions Structured group games
Needs Assessment	Entrance surveys Wandering flip charts Posing key questions
Presentations	Briefings about new developments Briefings about new products Training sessions
Information Sharing	Updates by participants
Planning	Visioning/goal setting Environmental scans SWOT analysis Stakeholder focus groups Benchmarking Strategy development Implementation planning

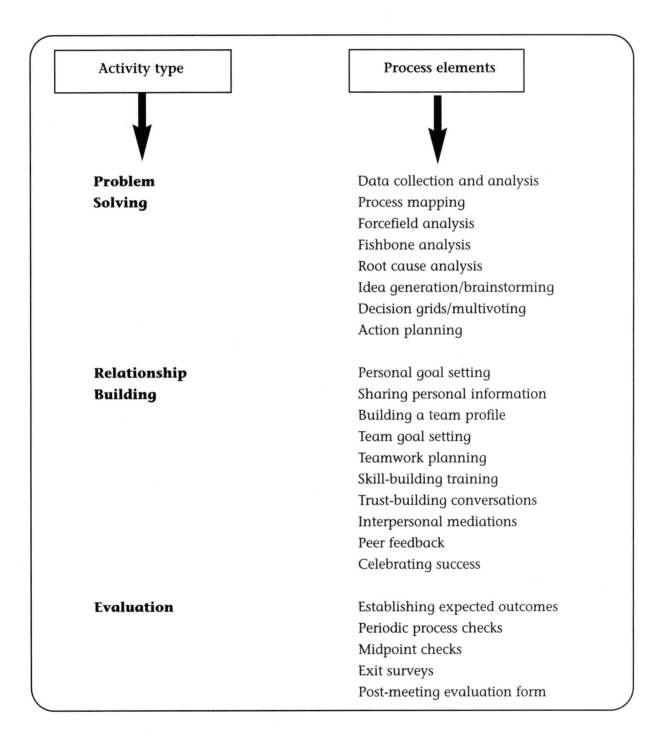

Activity type	Process elements
Problem Solving	Data collection and analysis
	Process mapping
	Forcefield analysis
	Fishbone analysis
	Root cause analysis
	Idea generation/brainstorming
	Decision grids/multivoting
	Action planning
Relationship Building	Personal goal setting
	Sharing personal information
	Building a team profile
	Team goal setting
	Teamwork planning
	Skill-building training
	Trust-building conversations
	Interpersonal mediations
	Peer feedback
	Celebrating success
Evaluation	Establishing expected outcomes
	Periodic process checks
	Midpoint checks
	Exit surveys
	Post-meeting evaluation form

Session Design Template

Outline the activities that will make up the facilitated meeting. Note that specific examples of meeting designs featuring process notes are provided in the Sample Process Designs section on the accompanying CD.

Agenda Items	Process Notes
Name: Purpose: Outcome: Time:	
Name: Purpose: Outcome: Time:	
Name: Purpose: Outcome: Time:	
Name: Purpose: Outcome: Time:	
Name: Purpose: Outcome: Time:	
Name: Purpose: Outcome: Time:	
Name: Purpose: Outcome: Time:	

Design Checklist

Use the following checklist to test your draft design:

___ Is the purpose of the meeting clear? Does this purpose reflect the input received from participants and key stakeholders?

___ Are there detailed expected outcomes for each agenda item?

___ Have potential blocks and barriers been identified? Are there strategies to deal with them?

___ Does the design include questions that enroll the participants in identifying personal needs and actively buying in to the session?

___ Have you created the targeted norming questions that are needed to set the right climate and ensure that you have the authority you need?

___ Have you categorized each topic as to its type?

___ Have you analyzed each discussion to identify which are decision-making and which are not?

___ Have you identified the specific tools that are needed for each topic?

___ Do you have alternative processes in mind if a mid-course shift is needed?

___ Have you anticipated the dysfunctional behaviors that may crop up by rehearsing what you might say to intervene effectively?

___ Have you realistically allocated the time needed to complete each discussion?

___ Have you included a midpoint check to ensure the process is working and on track?

___ Have you created a design that includes a good blend of presentations and participative activities?

___ Is the design well paced to allow for breaks and team activities that reenergize the group?

___ Have you allowed adequate time at the end of the session to do detailed forward planning?

___ Does the agenda include an exit survey or post-workshop evaluation?

Stage 3 – Contracting

One of the key steps in the consulting process is the contracting step. This step is especially critical for facilitators because it officially sanctions the assignment. It's also important because it's the step during which the facilitator has an opportunity to negotiate for the power needed to manage the assignment.

Contracting is also important in gaining buy-in. Even when participants indicate their desire to attend a particular meeting, it's still important to gain member buy-in. The activities that make up the contracting step achieve this through meetings with group members to preview and ratify the proposed process design.

How This Step Typically Unfolds:

- The facilitator circulates a summary of the assessment data and a draft meeting design to the clients.
- The parties meet to review the data and the proposed design.
- Any needed adjustments are made and the agenda is ratified.
- The facilitator and client identify the terms surrounding the assignment.
- The facilitator prepares a written letter of agreement to be signed by the client.

Purpose of This Step:

- submit a summary report draft design to the client
- gain participant input and ratification
- set mutual expectations, clarify roles and establish boundaries for the meeting
- discuss the challenging aspects and mutually develop contingencies

Activities:

- submitting a proposed agenda
- presenting the draft agenda to the participants/stakeholders
- accommodating member reactions and suggestions
- making adjustments and reaching agreement about the design
- negotiating your role and asking for specific authorities
- writing and sending a letter of agreement

Challenges:

- sharing sensitive assessment data in a totally neutral and professional manner
- creating an effective design that's based on the data and that meets critical client needs
- dealing tactfully with unrealistic client expectations

- managing the resistance of clients who reject important elements in the design
- being tactful and appropriately assertive when presenting the more challenging elements of the design

What Can Go Wrong:

- failing to focus on the important needs of the situation
- going along with a meeting design that members want but don't need
- proposing any activity that's too sensitive or difficult for members to handle
- not listening to client input and suggestions
- failing to uncover hidden agenda items or challenge assumptions
- failing to identify role boundaries and negotiate the power needed to facilitate effectively
- failing to identify and then manage client resistance effectively
- going ahead with a watered-down design that doesn't achieve the stated goals

Reasons to Leave the Facilitation Assignment at This Time*:

- The client rejects key elements of the design or waters down the design to the point where the meeting will likely be a meaningless exercise.
- The client does not assume responsibility for their role.
- The client does not grant the facilitator authority needed in order to be effective.
- The needed support mechanisms are not put in place to support implementation.
- Unrealistic time frames or other constraints are imposed without facilitator input.

*While leaving an assignment at this stage can be somewhat awkward, it's far worse to proceed to the next step and lead a facilitation in which the above circumstances are present. Meetings that contain no real possibility for success will only build cynicism and tarnish your reputation in the long term.

Proposing a Process Design

Once you have completed the assessment and design steps, it is important to share your findings with the client. This is typically done in two stages: sending a written report that includes a summary of the assessment data and a copy of the draft design, then meeting with the client to adjust the design and negotiate key elements.

If the meeting is relatively minor or if the client is far away, the contracting discussion can be conducted on the phone or even by e-mail. Face-to-face meetings are, of course, far better for building buy-in and creating rapport.

Even when only one person contacted you originally, it is always best to include a number of participants in the review process. This helps ensure the validity of the design and guards against taking the advice of just one individual whose views may not reflect a broad consensus.

Here are some ideas about what should be part of the contracting meeting:

1. **Share the original statement of request.** Summarize what you were told was the original purpose of the meeting. Keep this very simple.

2. **Give a data summary.** Share a very brief summary of the data that were collected. Don't provide more than you need to justify your design. Never reveal who said what during interviews.

3. **Review the design.** Explain the overall design principles that you followed. Review each item on the agenda, the rationale for each discussion, and the expected outcomes. Explain the specific process tools that will be used to address each item.

4. **Ask for feedback.** Invite members to share their reaction to the proposed activities. To overcome member reluctance to critique your design, use a pros and cons approach. You might ask:

   - What are the strengths of the design?
   - What are the weaknesses of the design/what concerns you?
   - What's missing/what's been overlooked?
   - What could challenge us or go wrong?
   - What could be improved?

5. **Seek improvements.** Accept as many participant suggestions as possible. Help the client understand why some of their suggestions can't be included. Deal with any client resistance that emerges.

6. **Negotiate your role.** Identify the power and authority that you need in order to be effective. This can include the appropriateness of making verbal interventions and ultimate control over the process elements.

7. **Clarify all parameters.** Identify what is expected of each party. Clarify any homework that participants need to do in preparation of the meeting. Review budgets, fees, and logistics like the date, location, and times.

8. **Next steps.** Review any next steps. Indicate that you will be sending the client a letter of agreement that summarizes the key parameters. Thank the members for their input. Express optimism that the meeting will be successful.

After the meeting, finalize your meeting design, prepare the letter of agreement, and send a pre-workshop package to the client.

Dealing with Resistance

During the contracting meeting it's very common for the client to resist one or more key design elements. Facilitators need to be aware of this probability and have strategies ready to deal with it.

There is a wide range of reasons why a client might resist or even reject proposed agenda items:

- Your data collection may be incomplete.
- Your assessment may be wrong.
- The client may be unwilling to face a serious problem, confront specific problems or deal with difficult people.
- Group members may feel threatened by the depth of some proposed conversations.
- Members may be unwilling to follow through on the action steps that are likely to emerge from the proposed initiative.
- Problem individuals may try to block to satisfy their personal agenda.

If it turns out that you didn't collect enough information or that you made an incorrect assessment, the input received during a contracting session can help stop you from planning an inappropriate intervention.

If, on the other hand, group members resist because they feel that the proposed activities are too risky or sensitive, the contracting meeting is the ideal time to surface this concern. The best way to deal with reluctance is always to ask members to identify their concerns and the conditions under which they would be willing to go ahead with what you propose. Their input will help you design the targeted norming questions that will help create the environment that is needed.

If you suspect members are resisting purely as an avoidance strategy, you may need to take a more assertive approach. Listen actively to the reasons a specific item is being rejected. Paraphrase what you hear, even if you totally disagree. Then firmly repeat what you think they need to do. Sometimes it's important to stand your ground on key design elements. Remember that there's often a gap between what clients want and need and that a facilitator contributes most when they help clients do what's really needed, not just what makes them comfortable!

One of the legitimate reasons to decline a facilitation assignment is if the client refuses to do what's really needed or if they propose activities that are likely to be counterproductive.

Characteristics of a Strong Contract

At the end of a successful contracting discussion:

- Everyone is satisfied that the design is based on sound data.
- All parties feel a high level of commitment to the activities described.
- The details – i.e., time, place, roles, preparation – are clear.
- Roles are clear and the facilitator has been given the authority they need to manage discussions effectively.
- The client has taken responsibility for their part of the initiative.
- Anxieties and possible risks have been openly discussed.
- The members and facilitator have positive feelings about each other.

A Contract Is Weak When:

- the intervention design isn't supported by the data collected
- the group's ability to invest the time required and commitment to follow through are in question
- the initiative is a low priority because of time and work pressures
- the members or the leader are trying to abdicate major responsibility to the facilitator
- it feels like members aren't openly discussing their concerns and reservations
- people don't trust the competence or personality of the person intervening

Putting It in Writing

Once there's a verbal agreement about the nature of the intervention, it's important to summarize key points in a brief memo. This lessens the possibility of misunderstandings later on. The memo doesn't have to be more than a page or two and should include:

- background to the request
- data assessment
- agreed-to approach and activities
- parameters and constraints
- timeframe and schedule
- expected result
- role clarification
- next step
- closing comments

Sample Letter of Agreement

To: All members of the Order Fulfillment Team

Further to our meeting, the following summarizes our discussions about the upcoming meetings. Would you please sign both copies and return one to me at your earliest convenience.

Background to this Initiative – The Order Fulfillment Project Team was formed within the Finance Department two years ago to expedite the processing of orders generated by the company's top 10 customers. The team worked effectively for most of that time, but lately the team has had difficulty remaining focused and implementing improvements.

Data Assessment – Member interviews and a survey have revealed the following:

- organizational priorities stated at the start of this process improvement effort have shifted
- the project budget and number of staff have both been reduced
- members have become unclear about their roles and responsibilities
- workloads among remaining members is unevenly distributed and unrealistic
- there is growing slippage on meeting critical project deadlines
- team members are missing meetings due to competing assignments

Proposed Approach and Activities:

Session #1 – three hours – 12 team members

- comprehensive analysis of the current situation in order to identify both the internal and external issues, blocks, and barriers being experienced by the Order Fulfillment Project Team
- small-group problem-solving sessions to assess the root causes of three key issues as selected by the group
- creation of action plans to address issue, including development of strategies for seeking assistance and support from upper management
- clarification of roles and responsibilities needed to implement action plans

Session #2 – three hours – 12 team members plus project sponsors

- update on progress to gain upper management assistance and support
- continuation of small-group problem-solving discussions to deal with remaining issues
- identification of additional improvement strategies
- review and updating of project parameters
- review of current roles and responsibilities to adjust member workloads
- open-forum meeting with upper management sponsors to present revised parameters and gain their support for operational strategies

Parameters and Constraints – from our discussions I understand that:

- these meetings need to take place immediately
- there is no budget to take the meetings offsite
- these discussions must take place during the regularly scheduled team meeting

Time Frame and Schedule – the two three-hour sessions will take place from 7:30 to 10:30 a.m. during the team's next two regularly scheduled meetings: September 12 and 19, in conference room A of the main plant.

Expected Outcomes – at the end of these two sessions, the team expects:

- to have identified the root causes of the current problems with the project
- resolution of key blocks and barriers
- practical strategies for improving the project's operation
- increased support from upper management for the team
- a new set of project parameters that correspond with revised budgets and reduced staff parameters
- clarity about member roles and responsibilities
- balance in team member workloads
- a renewed sense of commitment to the project amongst both team members and upper management sponsors

My Role: to plan the meeting process, to circulate a detailed meeting agenda, to identify any needed data collection tasks, and to facilitate the two three-hour sessions.

Your Role: to arrange for all meeting logistics, to send out the agenda and data collection assignments, to invite upper management sponsors, to maintain contact with upper management sponsors, to transcribe and circulate all meeting notes and to follow through on action plans created in the meeting. It is also your responsibility to hold a follow up meeting six weeks after these sessions to assure that action has been taken on key recommendations.

Next Steps: I will forward the agenda and additional data collection assignments to the team office ten days before the first session. You will make all meeting arrangements and send out the agenda, data collection homework, and meeting notifications.

I have enjoyed meeting the members of this team and look forward to assisting you to make this team even more effective than it has been in the past.

Sincerely,   Proposal accepted by:

_____   _____

Step 4 – Implementation

Once a strong contract is in place, the stage is set for a successful meeting. Facilitators should always be the first to arrive at the meeting site in order to fine-tune the room set-up. Being ready in advance of the start of any meeting gives you an edge. It allows you to greet people one by one as they arrive and feel confident that everything you need is in place.

How This Step Typically Unfolds:

- The facilitator refines the process design and creates a detailed agenda and a letter of agreement.
- The agenda, along with the letter, is sent to the client.
- The facilitator checks all supplies and prepares flipcharts of information to be posted in the meeting room.
- The facilitator arrives early to set up the room.
- The meeting is conducted.

Purpose of This Step:

- to provide facilitation expertise as per the letter of agreement
- to help the client achieve their expected outcomes

Activities Can Include:

- finalizing the design
- sending the design and contracting letter to the client
- preparing flip charts
- acquiring materials and supplies
- arriving early to set up the meeting room
- establishing a positive climate conducive to effective interaction
- facilitating discussions
- conducting periodic process checks to monitor progress
- adjusting the design whenever a new approach is needed
- evaluating member satisfaction at the end of the activity
- ensuring that members leave with clear next steps and follow-up assignments

Challenges of This Step:

- setting the right tone and climate
- keeping people safe during all sensitive discussions
- skillfully challenging assumptions and surfacing hidden agendas
- keeping discussions on track and on time
- staying neutral and taking accurate notes

- adjusting the process whenever current approach fails to work
- keeping all members engaged and participating fully
- effectively making needed interventions throughout the proceeding
- maintaining the confidence of the group

What Can Go Wrong:

- failing to establish clear and realistic outcome statements
- neglecting to negotiate the needed amounts of power and authority
- failing to establish the specific norms that are needed to create safety and ensure active participation
- failing to identify resistance and negotiate buy-in from all members
- not noticing when team members have withdrawn their buy-in
- not noticing that people have dropped out and are no longer tuned in
- plunging ahead with the agenda even when there are signs that a particular process isn't working well
- not having alternative processes in mind
- neglecting to evaluate progress at the midpoint
- hesitating to make needed interventions to redirect dysfunctional behaviors
- allowing discussions to run over or go off track
- allowing individuals to hijack the proceedings to achieve their personal goals
- failing to keep accurate notes that reflect member input
- failing to make summaries that bring closure to decision-making discussions
- not allowing adequate time for development of implementation plans
- neglecting to evaluate the outcome of the meeting

Reasons to Leave the Facilitation Assignment at This Stage*:

- if group members change the purpose of the meeting and deviate into an unplanned discussion that's totally outside the scope of the original request that both parties agreed to pursue
- if members engage in excessively dysfunctional behavior that's totally counterproductive
- if members behave in a rude or insulting manner towards the facilitator
- if it becomes apparent that there is no sincere intent to achieve the stated goals of the session and that the session is being held to give the illusion that action is being taken
- if the intent of the session is altered to achieve a negative outcome that violates the values of the facilitator

*While it may seem unimaginable, there are some situations that are so dysfunctional that you may need to tell the client that you can't go on with the session. If this happens, it is important to identify the conditions under which you would be prepared to return before you step down or leave the room.

Starting a Facilitation

The following sequence of activities is suggested at the beginning of a facilitated meeting:

- Welcome participants to the session.
- Thank group members for the opportunity to assist them.
- Introduce yourself and give a brief personal background.
- Have members introduce themselves by name and perhaps position.
- Conduct a warm-up activity that fits the time available and activity focus.
- Review the original request for assistance that was presented to you.
- Review a summary of the data that were collected in advance of the workshop.
- Post the data summary notes on a wall.
- Clarify the goal and the specific objectives of the session.
- Give a brief overview of the agenda for the meeting.
- Specify time frames. Appoint a timekeeper.
- Answer questions and make any logical changes to the agenda.
- Clarify the role you will be playing as the facilitator.
- Clarify the roles to be played by any other members.
- Facilitate a discussion to create the specific norms that are needed for the session.
- Take care of all housekeeping items.
- Set up a parking sheet to keep track of digressions.
- If members will be making sensitive comments to each other, provide coaching on the kind of body language and wording that's appropriate for these exchanges.
- Proceed to the first item on the agenda after having clarified the purpose, process, and time frame for the item.
- Commence discussions.

During a Facilitation

Throughout discussion, facilitators always:

- paraphrase ideas continuously to clarify meaning
- make interventions whenever participants exhibit ineffective behaviors
- summarize periodically to bring people back into the conversation or to create closure to discussions
- maintain accurate notes and display these to keep discussion on track

Facilitators also conduct the following process checks periodically even if things seem to be going along fine:

- check the pace by asking members how the pace feels to them:
  "Is this session dragging or do you feeling rushed? What can we do to improve the pace?"

- check the process by periodically asking members if the approach being taken is working:
  "Is this approach working or should we try something else?"

- Take the pulse of members by continuously reading body language and by asking:
  "How are members feeling? How is the energy level?"

Ending a Facilitation

One of the greatest sources of cynicism about meetings is the lack of follow-through on commitments made at previous sessions. This can happen for a number of reasons:

- lack of sufficient time built into the end of sessions for detailed action planning
- creation of overambitious or unrealistic action plans
- failure to troubleshoot action plans to anticipate what can go wrong
- failure to identify the resources that are needed to complete action plans
- failure to follow up on actions

In order to overcome these pitfalls, use the following steps:

- Help the group make clear statements about what has been decided.
- Ensure there are detailed and realistic action plans with names, budgets, accountabilities and dates beside each step.
- Lead a discussion using the troubleshooting outline on the next page.
- Round up items not discussed at the meeting, including those on the parking lot, prioritize them, and discuss how to deal with them in the future.
- Help the group create the agenda for their next meeting that includes a bring-forward item to follow up on past actions.
- Decide on the format for reporting on implementation, i.e., written reports or verbal report-back session.
- Help members decide who will take the flip chart sheets for transcribing.
- Conduct a written evaluation of the session.
- Solicit personal feedback from participants.
- Clarify your role in the follow-up process.
- Say goodbye and thank participants for the opportunity to facilitate.
- Help clean up and be the last to leave.

Planning for Action

One firm rule for ending any facilitated discussion is that the client must leave with detailed action plans. These plans need to specify what will be done, how, when, and by whom. This will help ensure that members assume responsibility to ensure that actions are carried out and reported back to the group.

What	How	By whom	By when
(the action)	(key steps)	(person responsible)	(deadline)

Troubleshooting the Action Plans

To ensure that implementation steps are completed as planned, it is very helpful to also engage participants in a conversation to identify all of the things that could get in the way of following through. This conversation allows you to help the client anticipate barriers and create strategies to deal with each of the blockages.

Use the following questions to help identify trouble spots:

- *What are the most difficult, complex, or sensitive aspects of our plan?*
- *What sudden shifts could take place to change priorities?*
- *What organizational blocks and barriers could we run into?*
- *What technical or materials-related problems could stop or delay us?*
- *What people-oriented issues do we need to be aware of and deal with?*
- *In which ways might members of this group not fulfill their commitments?*

What could go wrong, block us, or change suddenly?	What actions do we need to take to overcome each block?

Step 5 - Follow-up

Follow-through on action plans is the weakest element of most initiatives. It's very common that lots of effort is expended at the front end, but, by the time the meeting has adjourned energies and attentions are focused elsewhere.

To further complicate the situation, most facilitation assignments end when the main discussions end. This is especially the case for external facilitators. This means that facilitators rarely have much control or involvement with the ultimate outcome of most of the meetings that they lead.

In view of this situation there are only two possible courses of action. Facilitators can either build follow-on work into their assignment or help the client create well-developed implementation and reporting mechanisms.

How This Step Typically Unfolds:

- The facilitator transcribes their flip chart notes.
- A summary report is prepared and sent to the client.
- The consultant holds a post-meeting debrief with the client to discuss the outcomes and opportunities for continuing collaboration.

Purpose of This Step:

- to check on the outcomes of the meeting
- to assess the post-workshop evaluation comments
- to offer the client feedback
- to receive personal feedback
- to identify how the facilitator might be helpful with implementation activities
- to discuss future facilitation needs of the client and maintain the consultant/client relationship

Activities Can Include:

- a written summary of meeting notes
- giving and receiving feedback
- a face-to-face visit with the client
- periodic calls to check on progress
- post-meeting debrief sessions at which members share updates on progress

Challenges of This Step:

- The client may fail to act on their plans.
- The client may fail to monitor or report on progress.
- You may have negotiated a role that ends with the meeting, leaving you with no ability to help the client with follow-through.
- If you're external to the group, you may not be kept informed about the implementation progress.

What Can Go Wrong:

- The client may fail to implement action steps.
- There may be no bring-forward system to ensure ongoing monitoring of action steps by the client.
- There may be a lack of honesty in the final written assessments.
- You may be out of the communications loop and unaware of what's going on with action plans.
- You may lack the authority to play a role in the implementation effort.

Reasons to Leave the Assignment at This Stage*:

- Professional facilitators guard their reputations by leaving assignments only once results have been achieved.
- Assignments are left only after a full debrief and evaluation by the client.

*It seems redundant to speak of leaving an assignment at this stage since it's essentially over. There are, however, exit issues in this step even if they're in reverse! Since most clients will assume that your role ends as soon as the meeting ends, facilitators often need to negotiate a continuing role to ensure that implementation takes place. This is especially critical for internal consultants who are facilitating in their home base and may be directly impacted by the consequences of poor follow-through.

Monitoring and Evaluating Results

Since the responsibility for implementing actions rests with the client, facilitators need to engage meeting participants in discussions that help them plan a thorough evaluation process.

Here is a partial list of some of the questions that may need to be included at the end of a facilitated meeting to ensure that there are monitoring and evaluation mechanisms in place.

- Help the group identify specific indicators of success for each objective and expected outcome by asking:

  What would it look like six months from now if each of our expected outcomes were to be successfully implemented?

Objective ➡	Expected outcome ➡	Indicators of success
➡		➡
➡		➡
➡		➡
➡		➡
➡		➡

- Help groups establish mechanisms to gather implementation statistics or other data.

- Ask participants to discuss how progress will be reported and how often:

  ___ written reports
  ___ verbal updates
  ___ debriefing meeting
  ___ e-mail updates
  ___ conference calls
  ___ other?

- Help participants identify who needs to be provided with update information: This can include upper management, key customers, colleagues in other departments, etc.

Reporting on Progress

Date: _____   Group Name: _____

Name of Initiative/topic: _____

Current Stage in Implementation: _____

Progress To Date

Specific Activities Completed   Results Achieved

_____

_____

_____

Activities Remaining

What still needs to be done?   By whom?   By when?

_____

_____

_____

_____

Comments:

_____

_____

_____

_____

Signed: _____

Meeting Evaluation Form

Please provide your *anonymous* evaluation concerning the meeting.

1. What would you list as the accomplishments of the session?

2. What did you personally like? What did you personally dislike?

3. Please provide some personal feedback to the facilitator concerning:

Things that he or she did well . . .

Things that he or she could have done differently/ideas to improve . . .

4a. What overall rating would you give today's session?

1	2	3	4	5
Poor	Fair	Satisfactory	Good	Excellent

4b. Please provide some comments to illustrate your overall session rating:

5
Essential Processes
for Facilitators

THE PRIMARY CONTRIBUTION OF ANYONE ACTING IN THE PROCESS ROLE is to provide structure that creates effective group interaction. The flow charts and notes in this chapter detail the steps in these common processes.

> **Advanced facilitators know the steps
> of the most pervasive processes
> and are aware of how they unfold.**

It's important to note that some of the processes described may be completed during a single facilitated meeting. An example of this is a one- or two-day team-building retreat in which all of the process steps are completed at the same time. In other cases, the process will comprise a number of facilitated discussions held over weeks or months. An example of this is a process improvement project or a major change initiative. In these instances, several facilitated meetings may need to be held within each process step.

Similarly, each of the processes that are outlined can be applied at either the micro or macro level. For example, problem solving can be done with a group of five or with a group of 50. Likewise, strategic plans can be created for a single department or for entire communities. In every instance, the facilitator needs to identify both the scale and the scope of the activity.

Since situations vary greatly in terms of their complexity and related organizational dynamics, these samples are offered solely as a high-level overview for quick reference. They all need to be more fully fleshed out and custom designed to fit specific situations.

The process maps that are provided are divided into three categories:

Planning Process

Strategic Planning

Change Management

Project Management

Benchmarking

Priority Setting

Problem-Solving Processes

Large-Group Problem-Solving

Process Improvement

Survey Feedback

Win/Win Negotiation

Relationship – Building Processes

Customer Service Improvement

Team Launch

New Leader Integration

Conflict Mediation

Coaching

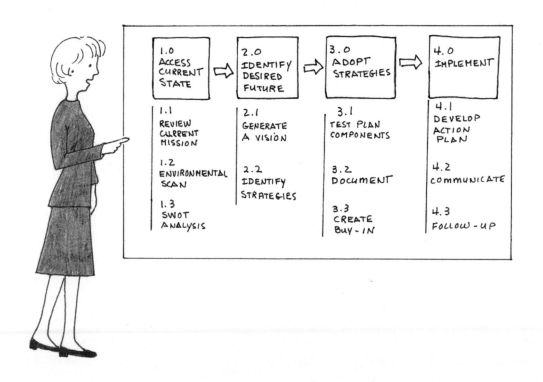

Strategic Planning

What is it? A participative process for creating long-range plans.

What's the purpose? To create a detailed multi-year plan with the input and collaboration of key stakeholders.

When to use it? When there is a need for a clear future direction, and buy-in from key stakeholders is essential.

Process Steps:

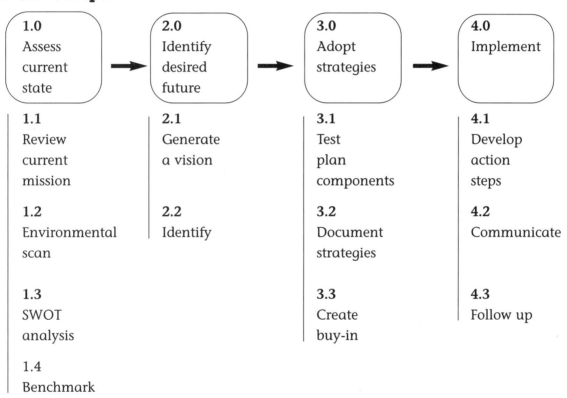

1.0 Assess current state	2.0 Identify desired future	3.0 Adopt strategies	4.0 Implement
1.1 Review current mission	2.1 Generate a vision	3.1 Test plan components	4.1 Develop action steps
1.2 Environmental scan	2.2 Identify	3.2 Document strategies	4.2 Communicate
1.3 SWOT analysis		3.3 Create buy-in	4.3 Follow up
1.4 Benchmark			

Strategic Planning – Process Notes

1.0 Assess the Current State

1.1 Review current mission – engage key stakeholders in revisiting the mission statement that has guided the organization in the past. Also review and assess the key strategies the organization has been using to achieve its mission.

1.2 Environmental scan – research the broader trends and patterns in the marketplace, the community, or the country. If the scale of the enterprise warrants it, hire consultants or futurists. In some scenarios, bring a large group together for an environmental scanning discussion. Highlight the trends most likely to impact the organization.

1.3 Conduct a SWOT Analysis – hold focus groups with key players to conduct a comprehensive analysis of the strengths and weaknesses of the current operation. Ensure that sufficient data is gathered to validate this analysis. Test analysis with stakeholders.

Next, explore the threats. Begin with current threats and current responses, then move on to discuss future threats and assess the effectiveness of dealing with them using current responses or strategies.

Finally, discuss opportunities. Start with current opportunities and threats, then identify future opportunities and assess the effectiveness of dealing with them using current responses or strategies.

1.4 Benchmark – study leaders and role models in similar or different enterprises. Conduct field research. Identify key success factors. Share this information with stakeholders.

2.0 Identify Desired Future

2.1 Generate a vision – engage stakeholders in visioning process. Encourage members to identify breakthroughs that represent departures from the past. Ask people to imagine the ideal future of the organization.

2.2 Identify strategies – articulate and flesh out the specific operational strategies that help the organization achieve the new vision. Distill key ideas and formulate a new mission statement.

3.0 Adopt Strategy

3.1 Test plan components – engage stakeholders in reviewing elements of the strategy to ensure feasibility (cost, feasibility, appeal to the marketplace, ease of implementation, etc.).

3.2 Document – prepare a written summary of the entire process including the new mission and strategies.

3.3 Create buy-in – share the new strategy not only with key stakeholders, but also other players who may not have been part of the process. Explain key features and deal with potential resistance factors.

4.0 Implement

4.1 Develop action steps – identify all of the specific steps that must be taken to execute the strategic plan. Assign responsibilities and align budgets.

4.2 Communicate – create suitable vehicles that communicate the plan appropriately to targeted audiences.

4.3 Follow up – create an evaluation mechanism for tracking and evaluating the effectiveness of the strategic plan.

Change Management

What is it? A series of steps designed to initiate and sustain a planned change effort.

What's the purpose? To engage those directly affected by the change to become engaged in creating it, rather than merely reacting to it.

When to use it? When major change is necessary and it's important to involve stakeholders to assure their buy-in and active participation.

Process Steps:

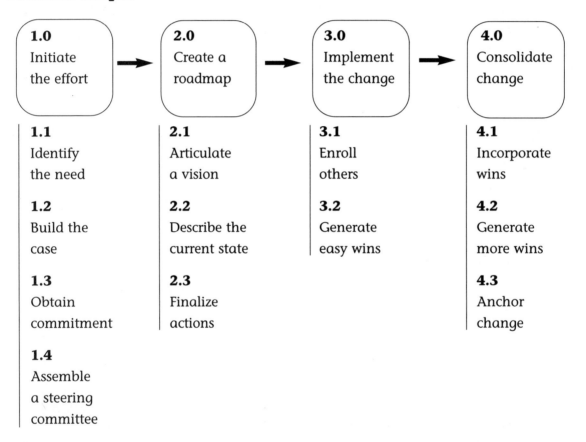

1.0 Initiate the effort	**2.0** Create a roadmap	**3.0** Implement the change	**4.0** Consolidate change
1.1 Identify the need	**2.1** Articulate a vision	**3.1** Enroll others	**4.1** Incorporate wins
1.2 Build the case	**2.2** Describe the current state	**3.2** Generate easy wins	**4.2** Generate more wins
1.3 Obtain commitment	**2.3** Finalize actions		**4.3** Anchor change
1.4 Assemble a steering committee			

Change Management – Process Notes

1.0 Initiate the Effort

1.1 Identify the need – the need for change is identified by a senior manager, a unit leader, or a team responsible for a specific product or process. The change initiator scans the environment, benchmarks against the competition, or documents the achievements of an industry leader to underscore the need for change.

1.2 Build the case – to overcome complacency, the change initiator may need to engage key decision makers in discussions about strengths, weaknesses, opportunities and threats (SWOT analysis). The change initiator may also need to collect and present data regarding performance levels and compare these to enterprise-wide standards of excellence.

1.3 Obtain commitment – the change initiator gains the unequivocal commitment of decisionmakers to support the change effort.

1.4 Assemble a steering committee – the change leader seeks the support of other organizational leaders whose active participation is needed in order to steer complex organizational change. This steering committee will serve as champions of specific change initiatives and typically includes experts who also act as coaches and advisers.

Third-party facilitators are typically sought at this stage to structure discussions and help manage the participation of employees, customers and suppliers.

2.0 Create a Roadmap

2.1 Articulate a vision – a clear picture of the end-state of the change process is created through facilitated discussions at various organizational levels. The features of the desired future are described in detail, including outcome measures.

2.2 Describe the current state – the corresponding current state is graphically described for each feature of the desired future state. Stakeholders are engaged in identifying the gap between the current state and future state. The need for change can also be surfaced by deploying forcefield analysis to identify the unproductive or ineffective aspects of the present operation.

2.3 Finalize actions – stakeholders brainstorm strategies to bridge the gap between the current state and the desired state. Detailed action steps, timelines, resources and sponsor support are put in place to ensure that the change effort is grounded and practical.

3.0 Implement the Change

3.1 Enroll others – the case for change and the change plans are shared broadly with those individuals who are likely to be affected by the change effort. These organization members are engaged in conversations to identify what's in it for them. They are invited to vent concerns and identify their resistance factors. Wherever practical and desirable, a broad base of participation is built for upcoming change activities.

3.2 Generate easy wins – if possible, quick wins are selected from the list of change activities to build momentum and strengthen buy-in to the change effort. Early wins are documented and celebrated.

4.0 Consolidate Change

4.1 Incorporate wins – add the principles and methods that are part of the change effort to the organization's rules, procedures and norms. Communicate these changes. Alter the organization's reward structure to recognize the change agents at every level.

4.2 Generate more wins – systematically implement various change initiatives. Document the efforts of staff. Bring staff together to share lessons learned and to disseminate best practices. Keep senior management champions engaged in helping, coaching and rewarding staff efforts to implement change.

4.3 Anchor change – continue to document the new ways. Promote successful adapters. Update administrative manuals and processes to reflect the changes. Provide formal training to share the key skills involved in the change effort. Follow through on the entire change process, taking care not to abandon it and shift abruptly to another change activity.

Project Management

What is it? A systematic series of steps designed to implement a specific program, manage an event, or develop a new process within a limited time frame.

What's the purpose? To coordinate the talents and energies of team members to efficiently and effectively achieve targeted results.

When to use it? To manage an initiative so that specific outcomes are achieved within a defined time frame.

Process Steps:

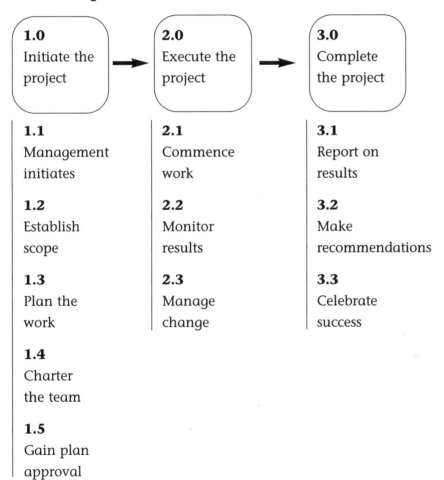

1.0 Initiate the project	2.0 Execute the project	3.0 Complete the project
1.1 Management initiates	**2.1** Commence work	**3.1** Report on results
1.2 Establish scope	**2.2** Monitor results	**3.2** Make recommendations
1.3 Plan the work	**2.3** Manage change	**3.3** Celebrate success
1.4 Charter the team		
1.5 Gain plan approval		

Project Management – Process Notes

1.0 Initiate the Project

1.1 Management initiation – sponsor identifies the need for the project. Initial parameters of the project are identified. Approximate timelines are set. Boundaries are identified. Preliminary budgets are created. Project team leader and members are named.

1.2 Establish scope – project team meets to review the initial scope and establish the specific goal of the project, as well as the measurable objectives. Customer/stakeholder needs and requirements are reviewed. Organization needs and requirements are also reviewed.

1.3 Plan the work – project steps are mapped and reality tested. Action plans that include detailed implementation steps are outlined. Preliminary timelines are refined. A detailed budget is created to reflect planned activities and anticipated costs.

1.4 Charter the team – the project team creates a team charter to define its operation. Charter details include behavioral norms, profile of member skills and member responsibilities to complete specific tasks.

1.5 Gain plan approval – the detailed project plan, revised budget and team charter are submitted to the sponsor/senior management for approval.

2.0 Execute the Project

2.1 Commence work – team members execute action steps in accordance with the detailed project plan.

2.2 Monitor results – members measure results using measures established during first phase. The team holds periodic meetings to discuss progress. Interim reports are prepared. Sponsors/key stakeholders are briefed on progress.

2.3 Manage change – the team monitors the environment to determine the impact of the project. Activities such as orientation events and skills training are held to ensure that others are able to accommodate and support the changes brought about through the project.

3.0 Complete the Project

3.1 Report on results – create a status report for sponsor/stakeholder review detailing the impact of the project, measurable results achieved, timelines and final cost expenditures. Also report on the long-term impact of the report on things like product innovation, market share, viability of the operation, cost savings, efficiency of key processes, customer relations and corporate image.

3.2 Recommendations – recommend additional activities needed to support the changes created by the project. Objectively identify any project failures and describe the lessons learned. Recommend any evaluations or other follow-up activities that should be conducted.

3.3 Celebrate success – review the results of the program and reward team members for their successes.

Benchmarking

What is it? A process for assessing and transferring best practice examples from other places.

What's its purpose? To identify, document and then transfer good innovations that are demonstrating their worth in other settings.

When to use it? As stand-alone activities or as part of strategic planning or process improvement initiatives.

Process Steps:

1.0 Set parameters	2.0 Conduct research	3.0 Analyze data	4.0 Implement
1.1 Identify objectives	**2.1** Analyze current operation	**3.1** Test data	**4.1** Plan for action
1.2 Define scope	**2.2** Select study target	**3.2** Prepare conclusions	**4.2** Monitor results
1.3 Create a team	**2.3** Collect data		

Benchmarking – Process Notes

1.0 Set Parameters

1.1 Identify objective – clarify the reason for the benchmarking initiative: is it to find innovative ideas, address a problem, streamline operations, or reduce costs?

1.2 Define the scope – identify the end-users of any innovations that are found; the budget, time frame and human resources available to implement them.

1.3 Create a team – find team members who have the technical or other skills that will be needed in order to conduct the benchmarking research. Also secure the support of a senior management champion who can assist with introductions to other organizations.

2.0 Conduct Research

2.1 Analyze current operation – collect data on the existing, ineffective process to uncover the details of the problem or performance gap for which innovative solutions will be sought. Map the efficiency, effectiveness and quality of current operations.

2.2 Select study target – use collected data to select specific processes or products that will be researched. Search databases, journals and professional associations for sources of potential best practice models. Gain permission to study the best practice operation.

2.3 Collect data – design and implement surveys, conduct site visits, interview best practice participants and observe models in action to collect data. Data may be collected about such elements as cost savings, time savings, flexibility, error reduction, manpower savings, product improvements and specific process improvements. Benchmarking can also be done to identify innovations in the area of marketing which looks at elements such as image, style, responsiveness, customer satisfaction and trend awareness.

3.0 Analyze Data

3.1 Test data – validate findings by checking and verifying information collected. Identify if the variables in the model organization are sufficiently similar to allow for valid comparisons and innovation transfer. Consider finding additional organizations where the same best practice can be tested to determine how it functions in different settings.

3.2 Prepare conclusions – determine the key principles, traits, or practices that form the core of the best practice. Assess the probable level of transferability. Identify the conditions required to support implementation. Recommend stakeholders.

4.0 Implement

4.1 Plan for action – create a detailed implementation plan that identifies the best practice that will be transferred, the measurable indicators of success, the timeline, the required resources, the names of those who will be accountable for implementation success and the names of the senior managers who will act as champions for the transfer process.

4.2 Monitor results – track progress throughout the implementation process and report to stakeholders regularly on outcomes. Recommend additional applications of best practices in the organization.

Priority Setting

What is it? A structured process for involving stakeholders in identifying priorities in a situation where budgets or programming must be cut back.

What's the purpose? To gain the knowledge and insights of the people most directly involved with the activity to be cut. To build buy-in to and acceptance of program reductions.

When to use it? When there is a desire to involve stakeholders in a sensitive cutback activity rather than having management determine priorities.

Process Steps:

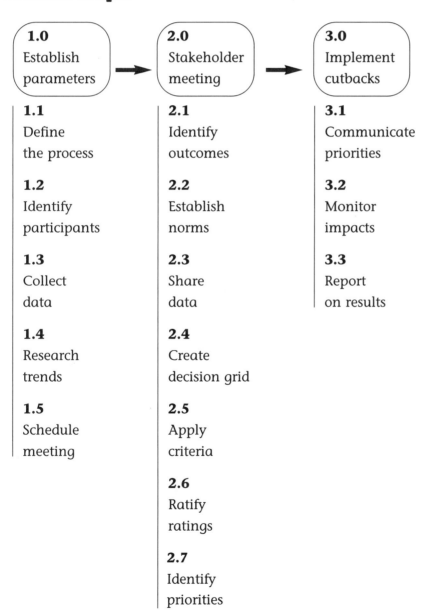

1.0 Establish parameters	**2.0** Stakeholder meeting	**3.0** Implement cutbacks
1.1 Define the process	**2.1** Identify outcomes	**3.1** Communicate priorities
1.2 Identify participants	**2.2** Establish norms	**3.2** Monitor impacts
1.3 Collect data	**2.3** Share data	**3.3** Report on results
1.4 Research trends	**2.4** Create decision grid	
1.5 Schedule meeting	**2.5** Apply criteria	
	2.6 Ratify ratings	
	2.7 Identify priorities	

Priority Setting – Process Notes

1.0 Establish Parameters

1.1 Define the process – describe the steps in the process of participative priority setting. Identify the benefits of involving staff in determining cutbacks to gain buy-in from senior management and also from frontline staff.

1.2 Identify participants – identify who needs to play an active role in the priority setting activity in order to give it validity and ensure buy-in to the recommendations. If there are too many stakeholders to allow for a manageable meeting (example: between 50 to 60), identify a core group. In these cases, create a mechanism such as focus groups or surveys to gather the input of the people who will not be at the priority-setting meeting.

1.3 Collect data – enroll the core group in collecting information about the current operation. In order to ensure consistent data collection, first identify the study criteria. Depending on the operation data can be collected on everything from the cost-benefit ratio of various programs or activities to the perception of customers concerning current products, programs or services.

1.4 Research trends – in order to make informed program or budget cuts, data is also needed about future trends, competitive forces, changing customer expectations and new technology.

1.5 Schedule meeting – once sufficient data has been collected and shared among all of the stakeholders, invite these critical individuals to a priority-setting meeting.

2.0 Stakeholder Meeting

2.1 Identify outcomes – openly share the negotiable and nonnegotiable aspects of the priority-setting exercise. Clarify the empowerment level of the group and the extent of the commitment that has been made by senior management to respond to the decisions of the group. Engage stakeholders in identifying the indicators of success. Ask: "Given the non-negotiables of this process, what would make you leave here today saying that this process has been successful?" List the indicators of success identified by group members and use them at the end of the workshop to measure the success of the process.

2.2 Establish norms – engage participants in discussions to identify the ground rules for the priority-setting exercise. Pose questions that set a safe environment and outline how sensitive topics will be handled. Synthesize member opinions and post the resultant norms to help ensure effective behaviors throughout all discussions.

2.3 Share data – ask for participants to make presentations of data concerning the programs, budgets, or structures facing cutbacks. Data about future trends is also shared.

2.4 Create decision grid – engage participants in building a decision grid to rank the existing candidates for cutbacks. Establish the criteria that will be used to rate the existing programs or activities. Criteria can include such elements as cost/benefit, importance to customers, support of strategic direction and cutting edge. Rank each criteria as high, medium, or low.

2.5 Apply criteria – once the criteria are ratified, small groups review and discuss cutback candidates, then use multivoting to identify a small-group priority ranking. Combine the rankings of the small groups to create an overall priority list.

If it's important to gain the buy-in of the total organization, all stakeholders can rank the cutback candidates using a survey or focus groups.

2.6 Ratify ratings – tabulate the rankings and feed results back to the core group or focus groups to ensure that the results are acceptable and valid.

2.7 Identify priorities – use the ranking to identify the high-, medium-, and low- ranked candidates for cutback activities. Engage the core group in interpreting the scores and in making detailed recommendations about the extent and nature of cutbacks. Ask stakeholders to create implementation strategies that limit the negative impact of cutbacks on customers, the operation, and staff in order to maintain high buy-in levels.

3.0 Implement Outbacks

3.1 Communicate priorities – report back to the stakeholders with detailed information concerning the ranking process and the implementation process. Implement cutbacks as per the plan.

3.2 Monitor impacts – identify critical success indicators and engage stakeholders in tracking implementation. Hold evaluation meetings to review the outcome data, identify both the positive and negative effects of the changes, and reflect on lessons learned during the process.

3.3 Report on results - generate a report that reviews both the effectiveness of the cutbacks and of the participative priority-setting process. Recommend further action.

Large Group Problem Solving

What is it? An application of the basic Systematic Problem-solving Model to accommodate groups of over 30 participants.

What's the purpose? Enables an organization to take a whole-systems view of a process or an operation. Creates buy-in and enrolls stakeholders in playing an active role in the implementation phase.

When to use it? When you want to involve all key stakeholders simultaneously in the overhaul of a process of operation that is in need of improvement.

Process Steps:

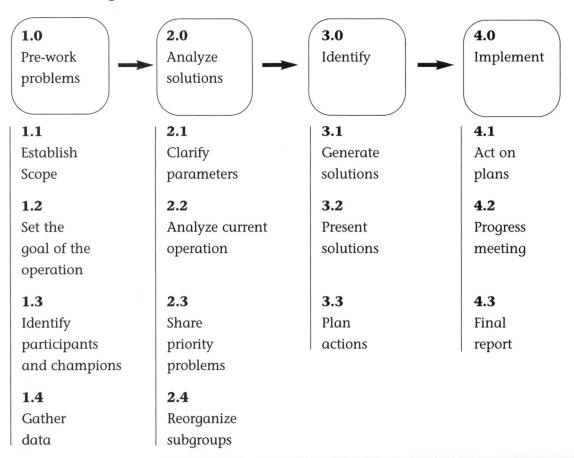

1.0 Pre-work problems	2.0 Analyze solutions	3.0 Identify	4.0 Implement
1.1 Establish Scope	**2.1** Clarify parameters	**3.1** Generate solutions	**4.1** Act on plans
1.2 Set the goal of the operation	**2.2** Analyze current operation	**3.2** Present solutions	**4.2** Progress meeting
1.3 Identify participants and champions	**2.3** Share priority problems	**3.3** Plan actions	**4.3** Final report
1.4 Gather data	**2.4** Reorganize subgroups		

Large Group Problem Solving – Process Notes

1.0 Pre-work

1.1 Establish the scope – the need for the problem-solving exercise is identified by a key stakeholder. A preliminary definition of the problem is created through conversation with various individuals who are aware of the current operation. Approval is gained to work on the problem with a large group.

1.2 Set the goal – after preliminary definition of the problem, the process owner identifies the goal of the problem-solving exercise.

1.3 Identify participants and champions –- based on the problem definition and preliminary assessment of the scope of the exercise, the process owner builds a small team of facilitators to help plan and lead the event. One facilitator is needed for every small group of 6 to 10 participants.

The facilitator team then identifies who needs to be involved in the problem-solving exercise. This may be mainly process participants, but can also include customers and suppliers who are external to the organization. The process owner also identifies from 5 to 10 upper-level managers to act as champions in support of implementation activities.

1.4 Gather data – extensive research is conducted to gather data in advance of the problem-solving meeting. This can involve such activities as documenting performance data, gathering cost/benefit information, conducting focus groups of internal or external customers and suppliers and mapping current processes. The data is summarized and shared with the participants.

2.0 Problem Analysis

2.1 Clarify parameters – once sufficient data has been collected, the large group of participants gathers for a full day of problem-solving discussions.

The process owner begins the event by making a presentation to the entire group outlining both the challenge and the goal of the exercise. The steps of the process are reviewed. Norms that encourage free speech and creativity are identified and accepted. One or more of the designated champions describes the empowerment being given to the group to make recommendations and expresses the support of upper management.

2.2 Analyze the current operation – after the large group presentation, the upper management representatives leave. The participants then adjourn for about 90 minutes to small-group settings in mixed groups. With the help of a facilitator, each group focuses on the entire process or operation. They use forcefield analysis to identify what's working well and then what is not working well with the current process or operation.

When the forcefield discussions are complete, each subgroup uses multivoting to rank their "not working" list. Each sub-group appoints a spokesperson.

2.3 Share priority problems – small groups return to the larger forum and sub-group spokespersons quickly review their group's "working" list and their prioritized "not working" list. While participants take a break, facilitators consolidate all of the "not working" lists. Duplicates are eliminated. Overlapping items are clarified and also consolidated.

2.4 Reorganize sub-groups – depending on the size of the large group, from five to ten of the top-ranked items are posted on the walls of the large room. Sign-up sheets are posted with each item allowing from six to ten people to join each group. When members return from their break, the priority items are reviewed briefly to ensure the right items have been selected. Participants are then invited to sign up for one of the problem-solving groups. Care is taken to insure that the right people join each of the problem-solving subgroups.

3.0 Identify Solutions

3.1 Generate solutions – the reconstituted groups adjourn to private settings and begin to address their assigned problem. With the help of the facilitator, members first conduct a thorough analysis of their problem. They then brainstorm solutions to their problem. An impact/effort grid is used to sort the solutions.

3.2 Present solutions – small groups return to the large room to take turns presenting their solutions. Upper-level managers who will act as champions return to hear the presentations, give on-the-spot approval to specific action steps, and offer to act as champions for specific initiatives.

3.3 Plan actions – once all of the subgroups have presented their action plans, received approvals, and gained needed upper-management champions, subgroups adjourn for planning sessions. Roles and responsibilities are identified for specific activities. Subgroup members write out detailed action plans for their assigned item(s).

4.0 Implement

4.1 Act on plans – At the end of the problem-solving day, facilitators collect the action plans and have them transcribed. A summary report is quickly prepared and circulated to all stakeholders. Implementation of actions begins immediately as per the plans.

4.2 Progress meeting – from six to eight weeks after the large problem-solving meeting, the process owner convenes a gathering of the stakeholders and champions. Participants meet for a few hours to share updates. Brief summaries are provided on the results achieved from completed initiatives. Work still in progress is also reviewed. Initiatives that are floundering are targeted for additional planning meetings to help move them forward.

4.3 Final report – the process owner monitors ongoing activities and tracks results. He or she communicates with all of the participants at regular intervals. When the entire activity is complete, a final report is produced that identifies the gains and lessons learned.

Process Improvement

What is it? A series of steps taken to improve the efficiency, effectiveness, and quality of any work process.

What's the purpose? To harness the wisdom of the key stakeholders in identifying problems and finding creative solutions.

When to use it? When there is a process that is underperforming.

Process Steps:

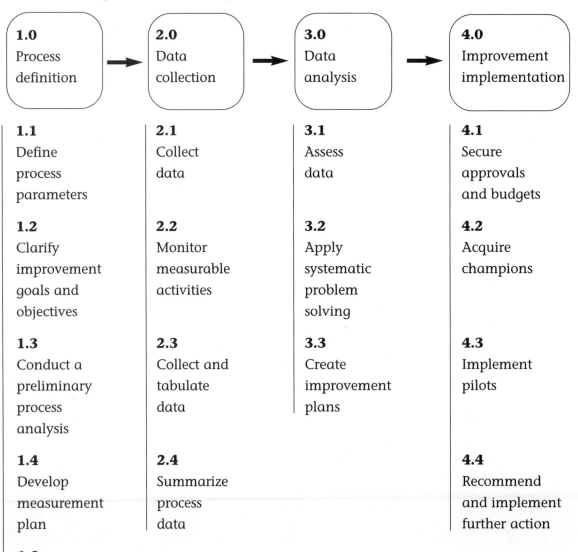

1.0 Process definition	**2.0** Data collection	**3.0** Data analysis	**4.0** Improvement implementation
1.1 Define process parameters	**2.1** Collect data	**3.1** Assess data	**4.1** Secure approvals and budgets
1.2 Clarify improvement goals and objectives	**2.2** Monitor measurable activities	**3.2** Apply systematic problem solving	**4.2** Acquire champions
1.3 Conduct a preliminary process analysis	**2.3** Collect and tabulate data	**3.3** Create improvement plans	**4.3** Implement pilots
1.4 Develop measurement plan	**2.4** Summarize process data		**4.4** Recommend and implement further action
1.5 Develop a data collection plan			

Process Improvement – Process Notes

1.0 Process Definition

1.1 Define process parameters – identify the process to be improved and describe all of the key features and steps of the current process. Use a top-down flow chart or activity-based process mapping to describe each step of the current process. Build this map with the input of key process participants and stakeholders to ensure the accuracy of the map.

1.2 Clarify improvement goals and objectives – identify the overall goal of the improvement effort. Write objectives that feature specific features of the desired end-state.

1.3 Conduct a preliminary process analysis – involve committee members and key stakeholders in discussions that yield a description of how the process currently works: key steps, timeline for each step, effective elements, weaknesses or problem areas.

1.4 Develop a measurement plan – create a set of performance measures to guide data collection. Identify the efficiency data to be collected such as unit/cost, manpower costs, and materials costs. Identify the effectiveness data you will collect such as the customer satisfaction input. Identify the quality information that you will collect such as durability of the process elements, reliability and breakdown rates.

1.5 Develop a data-collection plan – identify who will collect which data within specific time frames. Also identify how the data will be collected and reported. Create data-collection and recording mechanisms.

2.0 Data Collection

2.1 Collect data – study the current process and record information about costs, time, input, outputs, breakdowns, scrap, rework and common problems. Conduct surveys and focus groups of suppliers, customers, process participants, and senior managers to understand effectiveness elements. Benchmark against other processes or industry leaders.

2.2 Monitor measurable activities – set up studies that gather data about the process over a specific cycle. Monitor and record performance data using tools such as check sheets, control charts, histogram run charts and scatter diagrams.

2.3 Collect and tabulate data – gather data and create summary reports. Apply data-development software to help process information.

2.4 Summarize process data – create a summary report that describes the current state. Share report with key process participants and stakeholders.

3.0 Data Analysis

3.1 Assess the data – involve key process owners and stakeholders in meetings to assess the data. Identify key indicators of effectiveness. Use tools like fishbone analysis to identify areas in need of improvement. Use multivoting or a criteria-based decision grid to prioritize the issues, blocks and barriers.

3.2 Apply systematic problem solving – address the priority problems blocking the effectiveness of the current process using the steps of the problem-solving model.

3.3 Create improvement plans – involve key process owners and stakeholders in identifying improvement plans. These plans will include the action items from the problem-solving sessions plus the actions recommended from benchmarking efforts and stakeholder focus groups. Establish clear accountabilities. Identify timelines. Create mechanisms to follow up and evaluate results of improvement efforts.

4.0 Improvement Implementation

4.1 Secure approvals and budgets – ensure that improvement plans are adequately funded. Gain approval from senior managers, key stakeholders and important process owners such as suppliers and customers.

4.2 Acquire champions – approach at least one executive to act as champion for the improvement effort. This person will remove roadblocks, help secure special approvals, find additional funding and lobby important constituents.

4.3 Implement pilots – test the improvement strategies. Monitor and measure results. Monitor and evaluate results. Report on results to senior level management and to key stakeholders.

4.4 Recommend and implement further action – use pilot data to report on preliminary results. Refine improvement plans. Involve the process improvement committee in revising the implementation plan. Advise key stakeholders. Gain additional needed approvals. Secure additional funding if needed. Implement further action.

Survey Feedback

What is it? A group process that involves generating data, then feeding it back to group members so that they can interpret it and take action.

What's the purpose? Provides groups with a means for assessing their current situation or operation and provides a method for creating improvements.

When to use it? When data is needed to serve as a catalyst to create a compelling need for change.

Process Steps:

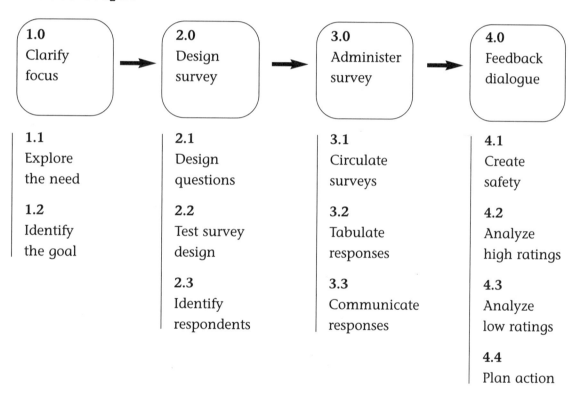

1.0 Clarify focus	2.0 Design survey	3.0 Administer survey	4.0 Feedback dialogue
1.1 Explore the need	2.1 Design questions	3.1 Circulate surveys	4.1 Create safety
1.2 Identify the goal	2.2 Test survey design	3.2 Tabulate responses	4.2 Analyze high ratings
	2.3 Identify respondents	3.3 Communicate responses	4.3 Analyze low ratings
			4.4 Plan action

Survey Feedback – Process Notes

1.0 Clarify Focus

1.1 Explore the need – help the client identify the focus of the survey. Surveys can be done to assess organization climate, employee morale, customer satisfaction, the quality of a product, the efficiency of a process, or the overall effectiveness of a team, to mention but a few. Conduct interviews and focus groups to engage various stakeholders in describing any problems or situations that may be part of the need for the survey.

1.2 Identify the goal – ask both the client and stakeholders to describe what they hope will be achieved through the application of the survey. What information do they hope will be uncovered? What improvements or other results would an ideal process yield?

2.0 Design Survey

2.1 Design questions – in response to the data collected, create a preliminary field of questions. Create more questions than are needed for the survey.

2.2 Test survey design – circulate the questions to stakeholders and ask them to review the questions to identify the ones that satisfy both the need and the goal of the exercise.

2.3 Identify respondents – interview product/process owners, key decisionmakers,and other stakeholders to identify who should complete the survey. Clarify whether responses should be anonymous.

3.0 Administer Survey

3.1 Circulate surveys – mail out surveys with clear information about how to return completed forms. If the survey is being administered using the internet or the organization's intranet, provide respondents with clear instructions about when and how they can respond.

3.2 Tabulate responses – collect surveys and tabulate data onto a single survey form. Do not interpret the results.

3.3 Communicate responses – share raw data with respondents.

4.0 Feedback Dialogue

4.1 Create safety – at the start of the feedback dialogue, engage participants in a conversation to create safety norms. Ask questions that lead the group to identify the conditions that will make them feel comfortable giving and accepting feedback. Ratify the norms and record them on a flip chart sheet.

4.2 Analyze high ratings – invite respondents to a meeting to review the survey data. First list all of the survey questions that received high ratings. Review each briefly and ask participants to identify why they believe that item received positive responses. Record these points.

4.3 Analyze low ratings – once the analysis phase is complete, turn attention to the responses that received low ratings and ask participants to identify why they believe these items received low ratings. Engage participants in generating ideas that will improve the ratings in each of the low-rated areas.*

*If the group is sufficiently large, divide participants into small subgroups of three to six individuals. Have each subgroup work on one of the low-rated items. This will make it possible to address a large number of issues in a short time and will add a degree of anonymity to the proceedings.

4.4 Plan action – hold a plenary session in which subgroups share only the improvement ideas. Use multivoting to identify the top three improvement ideas for each low-rated item. Ratify the choices and ask subgroups to develop action plans that include roles and responsibilities. Summarize ratified action plans and share the document with all respondents and stakeholders.

Win/Win Negotiation

What is it? A collaborative approach to negotiating agreements that aims to arrive at agreements that both parties can live with. Rather than the two parties bargaining as two opposing teams in a win/lose process, individuals from both parties work together as the members of one team to arrive at agreements that represents a win for everyone.

What's the purpose? To create long-lasting agreements that everyone has bought into and that represent a positive outcome for both parties.

When to use it? In situations where it is important that working relationships not be damaged by using a win/lose or competitive approach to bargaining.

Process Steps:

1.0 Prepare environment	2.0 Build team	3.0 Identify interests	4.0 Decide together	5.0 Implement	6.0 Monitor
1.1 Assess readiness	2.1 Charter team	3.1 Articulate interests	4.1 Analyze interests	5.1 Communicate agreements	6.1 Track results
1.2 Identify players	2.2 Set process goals	3.2 Rank Interests	4.2 Generate ideas	5.2 Trouble-shoot	6.2 Report results
1.3 Assess training needs	2.3 Clarify relationships		4.3 Sort Ideas		
1.4 Gain buy-in	2.4 Provide training		4.4 Record agreements		

Win/Win Negotiation – Process Notes

1.0 Prepare the Environment

1.1 Assess readiness – conduct a survey to identify whether the organization is ready to take a win/win approach to negotiating. Use the survey feedback process to engage participants in tabulating the results and identifying strategies to overcome low-rated items.

1.2 Identify players – identify who should be on the negotiating team and who is needed to act as champion to remove any blocks and barriers that limit progress.

1.3 Assess training needs – conduct a needs assessment to identify the skill development needs of negotiating team members and others. These can include things like: introduction to the principles of the win/win concept, meeting skills, dealing with conflict, effective group behaviors and group decision making.

1.4 Gain buy-in – bring key players together to affirm their commitment to bargain non-competitively. Facilitate conversations to create norms that set the climate for the win/win process and that build commitment to staying the course among both negotiating team members and other stakeholders.

2.0 Build the Team

2.1 Charter the team – bring the members of the negotiating team together to help them get to know each other, be briefed on how the win/win process works, review important parameters, and surface problem solve member concerns in order to strengthen member buy-in. The negotiation team also needs to develop a detailed set of norms that describe how team members will act during contentious conversations and other challenging situations.

2.2 Set process goals – to ensure that the process remains win/win and doesn't revert to positional bargaining, members need to discuss the characteristics of the win/win approach in great detail. Members need to commit to uphold these traits and use them periodically to test the effectiveness of the process itself.

2.3 Clarify relationships – members of the negotiating team engage in a needs-and-offers dialogue between representatives of the two parties to arrive at agreements about how the relationship will operate.

2.4 Provide training – implement learning activities in response to the training needs assessment conducted earlier. This may feature individual learning activities for team members or group workshops to build common skills. Since the win/win negotiation model emphasizes teamwork, team-building training will be an important component of this phase.

3.0 Identify Interests

1.1 Articulate interests – invite members to list the interests and issues that need to be addressed by the negotiating team. Ensure that each item is clearly understood and don't focus on whether or not people agree.

1.2 Rank interests – once all interests have been listed, identify criteria to rank these items in terms of how complex it is expected to be, how difficult team members expect it will be to find a mutually agreeable solution, and how much more homework the team needs to do before being able to tackle the item. Once each interest has been ranked as high, medium or low in each category, create a timetable for exploring each issue.

4.0 Decide Together

4.1 Analyze interests – start with the least complex and least contentious interest. Borrow the steps of the problem-solving process and facilitate a thorough analysis of the current situation.

4.2 Generate ideas – once an interest is clearly understood by all team members, use nonpolarizing group processes like anonymous brainstorming to generate a range of ideas that respond to the interest.

4.3 Sort ideas – use a criteria-based decision grid or an impact effort grid to identify the most promising ideas.

4.4 Record agreements – create a written summary of the agreement in each issue area.

5.0 Implement

5.1 Communicate agreements – hold forums to share information about agreements with all stakeholders. Create mechanisms for stakeholders to comment on the outcome, through either focus groups or surveys.

5.2 Trouble shoot – identify what can prevent the agreements from being implemented and work to develop action plans to overcome these barriers. Enroll champions to help overcome barriers.

6.0 Monitor

6.1 Track results – establish mechanism to evaluate results. Use a survey to gauge stake-holder satisfaction

6.2 Report on results – create a final report that documents the collaborative process, successes, challenges and lessons learned.

Customer Service Improvement

What is it? A series of steps taken to improve the quality of service to internal or external customers.

What's the purpose? To enhance customer loyalty through improved customer care.

When to use it? When there are complaints from customers, when the customer base is eroding, or to proactively improve customer relations.

Process Steps:

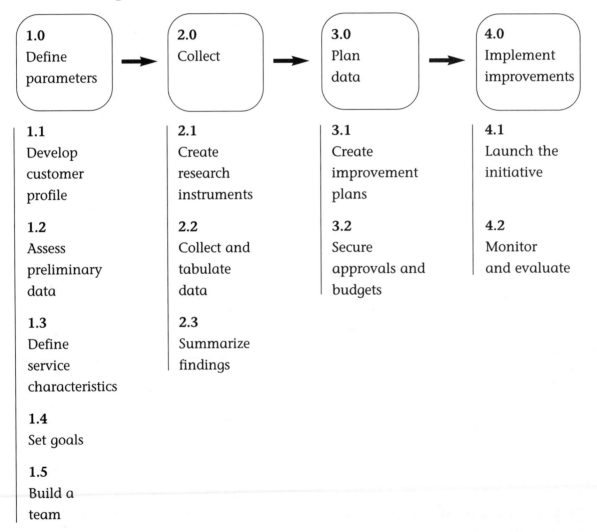

| 1.0 Define parameters | → | 2.0 Collect | → | 3.0 Plan data | → | 4.0 Implement improvements |

1.1 Develop customer profile

1.2 Assess preliminary data

1.3 Define service characteristics

1.4 Set goals

1.5 Build a team

2.1 Create research instruments

2.2 Collect and tabulate data

2.3 Summarize findings

3.1 Create improvement plans

3.2 Secure approvals and budgets

4.1 Launch the initiative

4.2 Monitor and evaluate

Customer Service Improvement – Process Notes

1.0 Define Parameters

1.1 Develop customer profile – identify the customer who is the focus of the service improvement effort. Clarify the reason for this choice, whether due to complaints about past services, desire to strengthen partnerships, or interest in creating new partnerships. Consult with those who have information or firsthand knowledge about the customer to gather preliminary data about the customer including: vital statistics, core values/beliefs, attitudes, social habits/norms, preferences, needs and expectations.

1.2 Assess preliminary data – rely on past knowledge about an existing customer to describe the challenges and issues that need to be overcome. For a new customer, conduct research into the general field to gather more information about that type of customer.

1.3 Define service characteristics – identify an overall goal to focus the improvement effort by defining the characteristics of excellent service. These characteristics will fall into two categories:

1) Procedural elements describe things like the standards of quality set for the products or services delivered, the timing standards, the process flow standards, the flexibility guidelines, communication standards, and guidelines about how problems will be solved.

2) Personal elements describe things like the appearance of the physical setting, the products, and the people, the attitudes displayed to the customer, the level of tact to be deployed, the approach to selling, and the manner in which customer needs will be handled.

1.4 Set Goals – use the preliminary data and the service characteristics as input to help identify the specific, measurable outcomes that need to be achieved through the initiative.

1.5 Build a team – identify the people who will work to conduct the customer service research and implement the findings. Where possible, identify team members who will remain in contact with the customers after the initial implementation phase. Also identify the upper-management representatives to whom the initiative will be reported and who are accountable for improvements.

2.0 Collect Data

2.1 Create research instruments – design the survey that will be used to gather input from customers. If focus groups will be used, create the focus questions and processes. If the preliminary data suggests internal production problems, put together process improvement teams to map existing processes to identify problems.

2.2 Collect and tabulate data – gather data and create summary reports. Apply data-development software to help process information.

2.3 Summarize findings – create a summary report that describes customer needs and delivery requirements. Share report with process participants within the organization.

3.0 Plan Improvements

3.1 Create improvement plans – involve team members and internal service providers in meetings to assess the findings and to make recommendations and create detailed action plans. Establish clear accountabilities. Identify timelines. Create mechanisms or ongoing monitoring and evaluation of the impact of service improvement efforts.

3.2 Secure approvals and budgets – ensure that improvement plans are adequately funded. Gain approval from upper managers. Gain buy-in from internal customer service contact personnel. If appropriate, test the plans with the customer.

4.0 Implement

4.1 Launch the initiative – create a marketing vehicle to put a face on the customer care initiative. Provide customer service skill training to contact staff. Make necessary improvements to internal processes.

4.2 Monitor and evaluate – set up mechanisms to track customer service activities against the service characteristics defined earlier. This can be ongoing interviews, survey forms, or monitoring of complaints and errors. Report on the impact of the improvement effort.

Team Launch

What is it? A series of structured conversations aimed at providing a new team with clear parameters and the opportunity to build a cooperative relationship.

What's the purpose? To set a clear framework for the team, to build buy-in and foster strong working relationships between members.

When to use it? To structure the first meeting of a new team.

Process Steps:

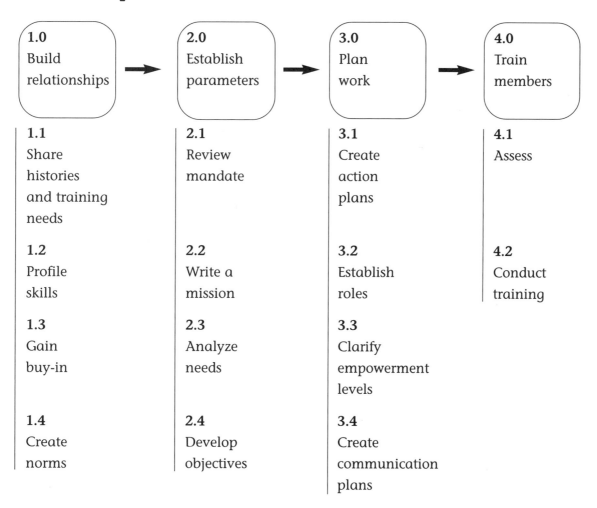

1.0 Build relationships	2.0 Establish parameters	3.0 Plan work	4.0 Train members
1.1 Share histories and training needs	2.1 Review mandate	3.1 Create action plans	4.1 Assess
1.2 Profile skills	2.2 Write a mission	3.2 Establish roles	4.2 Conduct training
1.3 Gain buy-in	2.3 Analyze needs	3.3 Clarify empowerment levels	
1.4 Create norms	2.4 Develop objectives	3.4 Create communication plans	

Team Launch – Process Notes

1.0 Build Relations

1.1 Share histories – invite members to share information about their background like education, work history, family life, hobbies, career goals, and personal goals in order to break the ice and build interpersonal rapport.

1.2 Profile skills – ask members to complete a personal skill profile in writing that can be shared with other members at the first meeting. This can include technical skills, communication skills, team leadership and people skills. This identifies the resources on the team and provides information for later work planning discussions.

1.3 Gain buy-in – invite members to share what they personally hope to gain from the new team. Ask how team success might help them achieve their personal or career goals. Ask how teamwork might enrich their work experience.

1.4 Create norms – engage members in a conversation about team norms. Ask specific norming questions that help the team identify how they will deal with differences of opinion, off-track conversations, or uneven participation. Record the team norms and post them in the meeting room. After the meeting, ensure that the norms are circulated to all members.

2.0 Establish Parameters

2.1 Review mandate – provide team members with all available information about the team, such as who created it, the reason it was created, the team's customers, the special challenges given to the team, expected results, the time frame for specific deliverables, the budget provided to the team, the expected duration of the team, and the overall level of empowerment given to the team.

2.2 Write a mission statement – engage members in the development of a specific mission statement that takes into account the team's parameters. Prompt the discussion by asking members to write a one- or two-sentence statement that describes what their new team is trying to achieve and what must be special or unique about their work. Have members do some individual thinking or work with a partner, then expand to the entire team. Record all key words and concepts; then assign the writing of the final statement to one or two members.

2.3 Analyze needs – assess stakeholder needs. Analyze the work that needs to be done. Create a detailed list of the challenges facing the team.

2.4 Develop objectives – create specific, measurable, time-sensitive objectives for all major activities. Include expected outcomes for each objective and time frame.

3.0 Work Planning

3.1 Create action plans – for each specific objective, develop action plans that identify what will be done by when and with what outcomes. Attach budgets and other resources to each item. Identify how each action item will be monitored and the reporting mechanism that will be used.

3.2 Establish roles – review member skills and goals. Identify the relative degree of difficulty and amount of work involved (high, medium, low) of each action item. Match team members with specific action items taking care to balance workloads as evenly as possible.

3.3 Clarify empowerment levels – for each action item, identify the degree of decision-making authority that is required for effective task management. Clarify if the team members are empowered to act without further approvals or if additional approval is needed on specific items. If more empowerment is desirable, make a case that can be presented to management to ask for the appropriate level of empowerment.

3.4 Create communication plans – identify who must be kept informed of the team's progress. For each stakeholder, identify whether they will receive written or oral reports and the nature and timing of those reports. Also identify timing and frequency of team meetings.

4.0 Team Training

4.1 Assess training needs – identify any skill gaps that exist in light of the objectives and action plans of the team.

4.2 Conduct training – arrange for individual team members to obtain the technical skill training that they require to execute action plans. Also arrange for the team to attend training together in such topics as meeting management, facilitation skills, and group skills such as decision making and conflict management.

New Leader Integration

What is it? A dialogue designed to create a bond between an existing team and a new leader. A communication process that encourages the sharing of expectations about goals, challenges, style and culture.

What's the purpose? To minimize disruption to team productivity by smoothly transitioning a new leader into an existing team. To accelerate the development of familiarity and trust between the new leader and the members.

When to use it? When an established team or department is about to receive a new leader.

Process Steps:

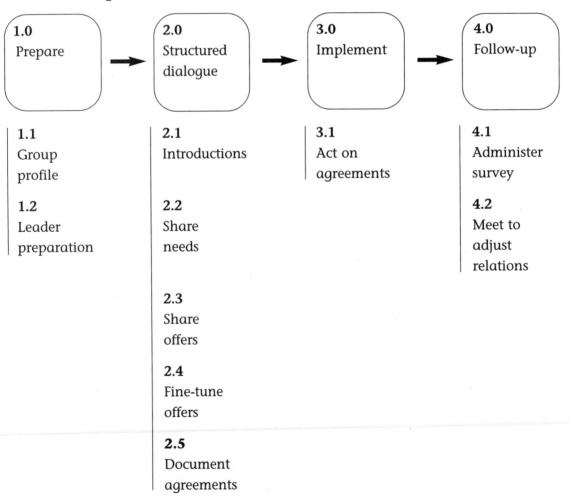

1.0 Prepare	2.0 Structured dialogue	3.0 Implement	4.0 Follow-up
1.1 Group profile	2.1 Introductions	3.1 Act on agreements	4.1 Administer survey
1.2 Leader preparation	2.2 Share needs		4.2 Meet to adjust relations
	2.3 Share offers		
	2.4 Fine-tune offers		
	2.5 Document agreements		

New Leader Integration - Process Notes

1.0 Prepare

1.1 Group profile – after the appointment of a new leader is announced, but before the leader meets team members, members meet to create a profile of their team. Among the things they discuss are: Who are we – our purpose, staff/skills, products/services? What are we doing well/what achievements are we most proud of? Why are we doing well? What aren't we doing well/what's blocking us from being effective? What are we doing to improve? What's ahead for us in the next six months, one year, three years? Under what leadership style do we work best? Why? What levels of empowerment have we been given for which specific activities? What empowerment levels do we need in order to operate effectively? What do we need from the new leader in order to be effective?

1.2 Leader preparation – once the group profile has been recorded, the summary report is shared in private with the new leader. The leader is given time to study the document and prepare a similar outline of his or her background.

2.0 Structured Dialogue

2.1 Introductions – the team and the new leader are brought together for a two- to three-hour meeting. Members introduce themselves and say a few things about their background. The new leader does the same. Each item of the team's profile is then reviewed and the new leader makes comments appropriate to each item. The blocks and barriers mentioned by the team are not solved that day, but are referred to a future problem-solving meeting.

2.2 Share needs – at the completion of the profile, the needs of the team and of the leader are reviewed. Both lists are recorded on separate flip chart sheets. The leader is given the team members' list of needs and leaves the room. While they're separated, each party discusses offers that they're prepared to make to each other. Each party records their offers on a flip chart sheet.

2.3 Share offers – the leader returns with his or her flip chart of offers and reviews each item. Team members then present their offers to the leader.

2.4 Fine-tune offers – after all of the offers have been shared, there is a discussion to ensure clarification and to suggest alterations or additions. The final offers lists are then ratified.

2.5 Document agreements – once all present indicate that they can live with the offers, they're typed and circulated. These lists of offers represent agreements about the relationship of the team and the leader.

3.0 Implement

3.1 Act on agreements – a period of three to six months is established during which the two parties will commence working together.

4.0 Follow-up

4.1 Administer survey – at the end of the prescribed period, the offers of each party are turned into a survey. Team members are invited to anonymously rate the extent to which the leader responded to their needs. The leader rates the extent to which the team has fulfilled their offers.

4.2 Meet to adjust relations – survey data is tabulated but not interpreted. The results are fed back to the team and the leader at a survey feedback meeting. Discussion at this meeting centers on identifying: Which items received high ratings and why? Which items received low ratings? Actions that could be taken to raise the ratings on any low items are discussed. The team leader may leave the room while the members deliberate. Improvement ideas are shared, ratified and documented. Parties leave the session with a commitment to act on their new agreements.

Conflict Mediation

What is it? A positive and constructive dialogue between two parties to resolve a dispute and clarify relationships.

What's the purpose? To generate mutual agreements and identify actions that can repair a strained relationship.

When to use it? Whenever there are tensions between two co-workers or between a leader and team members.

Process Steps:

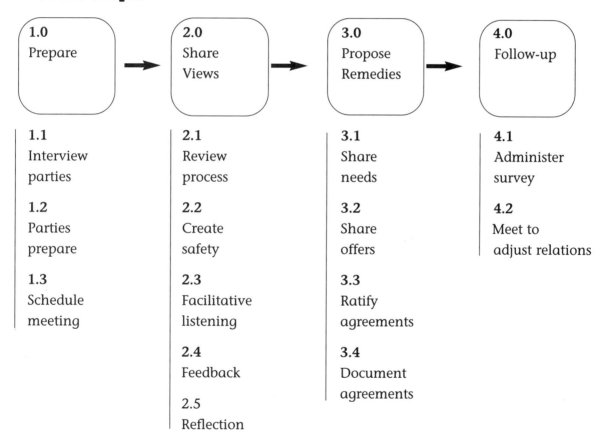

1.0 Prepare	2.0 Share Views	3.0 Propose Remedies	4.0 Follow-up
1.1 Interview parties	2.1 Review process	3.1 Share needs	4.1 Administer survey
1.2 Parties prepare	2.2 Create safety	3.2 Share offers	4.2 Meet to adjust relations
1.3 Schedule meeting	2.3 Facilitative listening	3.3 Ratify agreements	
	2.4 Feedback	3.4 Document agreements	
	2.5 Reflection		

Conflict Mediation – Process Notes

1.0 Prepare

1.1 Interview parties – contact the parties who will be taking part in the dialogue to inform them of the activity. Share the rules and process to reassure participants that this will be a positive and constructive conversation. If the parties are being ordered to take part to settle a dispute, be clear that this is a mandated conversation.

1.2 Parties prepare – schedule the meeting to allow sufficient time for the parties to reflect on their relationship or a specific conflict situation and make notes.

1.3 Schedule meeting – plan the meeting to be held at the end of the day so that participants can go home immediately afterward. Find a private location for the dialogue that is away from the parties' workplace. Make sure there is at least one additional room adjacent to the meeting room that can be used as a breakout space.

2.0 Share Views

2.1 Review process – when parties arrive, be friendly but firm. Post the notes below and review them:

> - One person will present his or her view of the situation.
> - The other person will not speak except to ask clarifying questions.
> - The listener must make notes about the other person's views.
> - When the first person is finished, the second person will give a summary of what he or she heard.
> - If the first person is satisfied that he or she was heard correctly, the process will be repeated.
> - At no point will anyone interrupt, interject, or argue.
> - Everyone will maintain neutral body language.
> - The facilitator can and will stop proceedings if any rule is broken.
> - Once both parties agree that they have been heard, there will be a recess during which each party answers two questions:
>   *"What I need from you to put this behind us . . . and*
>   *What I'm offering you in return."*
> - The parties reconvene to share their needs and offers and make a commitment to act on them.
> - All conversations will be kept confidential and not be shared with other group members.

2.2 Create safety – before parties speak, engage them in a conversation to set some guidelines for the conversation. Engage them in a conversation to create norms that ensure the conversations will be comfortable. Ask them to list the rules that make it possible for them to listen respectfully and with an open mind. Ratify the new norms with both parties and record them on a flip chart sheet. Post the new norms within clear sight of both participants.

2.3 Facilitative listening – randomly choose one person to present his or her views about the conflict situation or the relationship while the other person listens actively and makes notes. Strictly enforce the rules and make sure that people are displaying neutral body language and are asking only clarifying questions. Stop any rebuttals or arguments immediately.

2.4 Feedback – once the first person indicates that he or she has fully shared his or her view of the situation, ask the second person to paraphrase the points made by the first person. Reinforce the need to be neutral and calm when he or she paraphrases. At the end of the paraphrase, ask the first speaker if the other party has given a correct summary of the first party's points. If the first party feels satisfied, reverse roles and repeat the process with the second party.

2.5 Reflection – congratulate the parties for their willingness to hear the other person. Send the parties home to reflect on what they have heard. Tell them they must not call anyone else to share confidential information. Ask them to review their notes and reflect on what they need from the other person in order to restore effective working relationships.

3.0 Propose Remedies

3.1 Share needs – parties return to the second session and take turns telling each other what they need from the other person in order to restore effective working relationships. Each party paraphrases what the other party needs. Clarifying questions are allowed, but argumentative conversations are strictly avoided.

3.2 Share offers – the needs lists are traded and the parties adjourn to separate rooms to reflect on each other's needs. During this period of reflection, each party is to identify the actions it is willing to take in order to restore effective working relations. These offers are to be specific and in direct response to the expressed needs of the other party in the dispute.

3.3 Ratify agreements – parties return and read their offers to each other. Each party may ask clarifying questions. If an item is not acceptable, people are invited to restate their need and ask for a modification in the offer. Once the offers are accepted, they create the basis of an agreement and the meeting can end.

3.4 Document agreements – the facilitator arranges to have the offers typed and circulated to guide the parties as they work together.

4.0 Follow up

4.1 Administer survey – use the offers to create a survey participants use to rate the extent to which the other party met their needs.

4.2 Meet to adjust relations – parties receive the other person's ratings in advance of the meeting so they come to the follow-up meeting prepared to make further commitments that will satisfy the needs of the other party.

Coaching

What is it? A structured series of steps designed to encourage improved performance in an individual who is underperforming.

What's its purpose? Improved personal performance.

When to use it? When an individual's performance does not match job expectations and there's a desire to offer the person an opportunity to improve.

Process Steps:

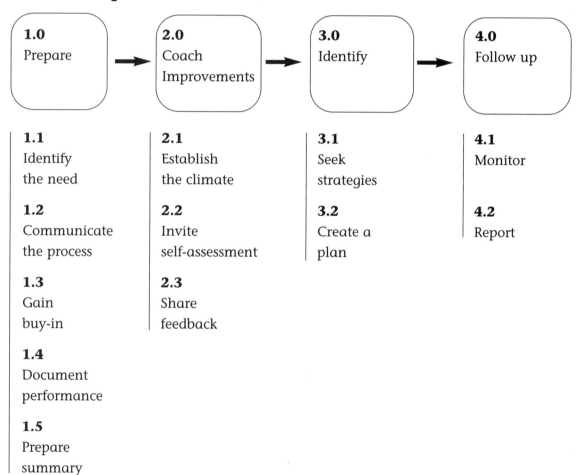

1.0 Prepare	**2.0** Coach Improvements	**3.0** Identify	**4.0** Follow up

1.1
Identify
the need

1.2
Communicate
the process

1.3
Gain
buy-in

1.4
Document
performance

1.5
Prepare
summary

2.1
Establish
the climate

2.2
Invite
self-assessment

2.3
Share
feedback

3.1
Seek
strategies

3.2
Create a
plan

4.1
Monitor

4.2
Report

Coaching – Process Notes

1.0 Prepare

1.1 Identify the need – this will be either at the request of the person seeking coaching or will be recommended to correct performance issues.

1.2 Communicate the process – meet with the person who will be coached to share the purpose of the process and to share the key steps so he or she can prepare. Establish a time to meet and find a suitable, private location for the sessions.

1.3 Gain buy-in – if the person is not seeking coaching, invite him or her to surface any resistance he or she may feel toward the coaching activity. Ask the person to identify the conditions under which he or she would welcome the coaching activity. Encourage the person to identify the potential upside of the coaching activity for him or her.

1.4 Document performance – keep specific detailed notes about the person's performance. This can involve such diverse activities as keeping a log of activities, observing the person performing his or her job, or reviewing the products the person produces. Documentation is needed in order to be able to give specific feedback concerning performance. The person who will be coached is also advised to maintain active records of his or her performance.

1.5 Prepare summary – write the specific, detailed summary of the key points about the person's performance on both a flip chart and on notepaper. This lets you refer to your notes during the coaching and also provides the member with a written copy to take away at the end of the session.

2.0 Coach

2.1 Establish climate – thank the person for coming and explain the purpose, which is to offer helpful performance feedback. Explain that your approach will be confidential, supportive, and in partnership with them. Inform the participant that your approach will consist of giving specific feedback and then helping them seek improvements. Clarify the expected outcome: namely that the person being coached will leave the session with specific plans for professional improvement.

2.2 Invite self-assessment – name the general area of concern and invite the person to give his or her perception of how he or she is performing. Listen actively to determine the person's level of self-awareness and openness to change. Paraphrase his or her key points.

2.3 Share feedback – express empathy about how hard it is to receive feedback. Request that the person listen to you without interrupting or becoming defensive. Limit the person to asking questions of clarification.

Provide your feedback in a totally factual, objective manner. Without attributing motives or personalizing any of the comments, tell the person what he or she did, when, and the impact of his or her actions. Answer all specific questions the person may have.

If the person seems to be denying or resisting the information, firmly restate and then ask him or her to paraphrase what he or she is hearing you say. It is not essential that the person agrees with the feedback, only that they accurately heard it.

The person receiving coaching may need a break to digest the input that he or she has received and identify improvement strategies. If so, adjourn until another day to allow the person to develop improvement ideas.

3.0 Identify Improvements

3.1 Seek solutions – invite the person to identify solutions. Be as supportive as possible of his or her suggestions, since the most effective ideas are always those made by the person being coached. If these suggestions are inadequate given the situation, assertively describe the expected standard of performance in specific detail. Answer any question about what is expected. Be open to making all reasonable amendments.

3.2 Create a plan – record any action plans that have been discussed. Set clear time frames on all improvement activities. Help the person identify and locate any training that he or she needs. Offer ongoing mentoring support.

3.0 Follow-up

3.1 Monitor – describe a specific monitoring and report back process. This could include additional coaching meetings. It also often features written documentation. Set a specific timetable for ongoing monitoring and coaching activities. Make sure they know exactly when and how you'll be following up. Compliment or otherwise reward the willingness of the team member to improve his or her performance.

3.2 Report – provide the organization with whatever written summary is required in order to document the performance improvement effort.

Notes

References

Chapter 1 – Advanced Strategies Overview

Axelrod, R., Dannemiller, K., Loup, R., and Jacob, R. *Real Time Strategic Change: A Consultant's Guide to Large Scale Meetings.* (1994) Dannemiller Tyson Associates. Ann Arbor, MI.

Beckhard, R. *Organization Development: Strategies and Models.* (1969) Addison-Wesley. Reading, MA.

Bradford, L. P., ed. *Group Development.* (1978) University Associates. San Diego, CA.

Brockett. R. G., ed. *Ethical Issues in Adult Education.* (1998) Teachers College Press. New York, NY.

Burke, W. *Organization Development: Principles and Practices.* (1980) Little, Brown & Company. New York, NY.

Cooper, S., and Heenan, C. *Preparing, Designing and Leading Workshops: A Humanistic Approach.* (1980) CBI Publishing Company Inc. Boston, MA.

French, W., and Bell, C., Jr. *Organization Development: Behavioral Science Interventions for Organization Improvement.* 3rd ed. (1990) Prentice-Hall. Englewood Cliffs, NJ.

Heron, J. *Group Facilitation: Theories and Models for Practice.* (1993) Kogan Page. London, UK.

Laborde, G. *Influencing with Integrity.* (1984) Syntony Publishing. Palo Alto, CA.

Likert, R. *New Patterns of Management.* (1967) McGraw-Hill. New York, NY.

Mosvick, R., & Nelson, R. *We've Got to Start Meeting Like This!* (1987) Scott, Foresman and Company.

Rees, F. *The Facilitator Excellence Handbook.* (1998) Jossey-Bass/Pfeiffer. San Francisco, CA.

Stanfield, R. B., ed. *The Art of Focused Conversation.* (2000) ICA Canada. Toronto, Canada.

Strachen, D. *Questions that Work.* ST Press. (2001) Ottawa, Canada.

Weaver, R. G., and Farrell, J. D. *Managers as Facilitators.* (1997) Berrett-Koehler. San Francisco, CA.

Chapter 2 – The Complexities of Decision Making

Adams, J. L. *Conceptual Blockbusting.* (1974) W.H. Freeman. San Francisco, CA.

Avery, M., Auvine, B., Streibel, B., and Weiss, L. *Building United Judgement: A Handbook for Consensus Decision Making.* (1981) Center for Conflict Resolution. Madison, WI.

Axelrod, R. *The Evolution of Cooperation.* (1984) Basic Books. New York, NY.

Fisher, A .B. *Small Group Decision Making: Communication and Group Process.* (1974) McGraw-Hill. New York, NY.

Fisher, R., and Ury, W. *Getting to Yes.* (1991) Penguin Books. New York. NY.

Hart, L. B. *Faultless Facilitation.* (1992) H.R.D. Press, Amherst, MA.

Howell, J. L. *Tools for Facilitating Team Meetings.* (1995) Integrity Publishing. Seattle, WA.

Kaner, S. *Facilitator's Guide to Participatory Decision-Making.* (1996) New Society Publishers, Philadelphia, PA.

Kayser, T. A. *Mining Group Gold.* (1990) Serif Publishing. Sequido, CA.

Levine, S. *Getting Resolution: Turning Conflict into Collaboration.* (1999) Berrett-Koehler. San Francisco, CA.

Maier, R. K. *Problem-Solving Discussions and Conferences.* (1963) McGraw-Hill, New York, NY.

McPherson, J. H. *The People, the Problems, and the Problem-Solving Methods.* (1967) The Pendell Company. Midland, MI.

Saint, S., and Lawson, J. R. *Rules for Reaching Consensus.* (1994) Jossey-Bass/Pfeiffer. San Francisco, CA.

Taglere, D. A. *How to Meet, Think and Work to Consensus.* (1992) Pfeiffer & Company. San Diego, CA.

Van Gundy, A. B. *Techniques of Structured Problem Solving.* (1981) Van Nostrand Reinhold. New York, NY.

Vengel, A. *The Influence Edge: How to Pursuade Others to Help You Achieve Your Goals.* (1998) Berrett-Koehler. San Francisco, CA.

Chapter 3 – Conflict Management Strategies

Argyris, C. *Intervention Theory and Method.* (1970) Addison-Wesley. Reading, MA.

Beckhard, R. "The Confrontation Meeting." (1967) *Harvard Business Review*: #45. Boston, MA.

Bens, I. *Facilitating With Ease!* (2005) Jossey-Bass. San Francisco.

Blake, R. R., Shepard, H., and Mouton, J. S. *Managing Intergroup Conflict in Industry.* (1965) Gulf Publishing. Houston, TX.

Cloke, K., and Goldsmith, J. *Resolving Conflicts at Work.* (2001) Jossey-Bass. San Francisco, CA.

de Bono, E. *I am Right, You are Wrong.* (1990) Viking Press. New York, NY.

Deutsch, M., and Coleman, P. T., eds. *Handbook of Conflict Resolution.* (2002) Jossey-Bass. San Francisco, CA.

Dimock, H. G. *Leadership and Group Development.* (1986) University Associates. San Diego, CA.

Eggleton, C. H., and Rice, J. C. *The Fieldbook of Team Interventions.* (1996) H.R.D. Press. Amherst, MA.

Eiseman, J. W. "*Reconciling Incompatable Positions.*" (1978) *Journal of Applied Behavior Science.* 14, 133–150.

Forsyth, D. R. *Group Dynamics.* (1990) Brooks/Cole. Pacific Grove, CA.

Francis, D., and Young, D. *Improving Work Groups: A Practical Manual for Team Building.* (1992) Pfeiffer and Company. Toronto, Canada.

Hunsaker, P., and Alessandra, A. *The Art of Managing People.* (1980) Prentice-Hall. New York, NY.

Keating, C. J. *Dealing With Difficult People.* (1984) Paulist Press. New York, NY.

Kindler, H. S. *Managing Disagreement Constructively.* (1988) Crisp Publications. Los Altos, CA.

Likert, R., and Likert, J. G. *New Ways of Managing Conflict.* (1976) McGraw-Hill. New York, NY.

Mosvick, R., and Nelson, R. *We've Got to Start Meeting Like This!* (1987) Scott, Foresman. Glenview, IL.

Pfeiffer, J. W., and Jones, J. E. *A Handbook of Structured Experiences for Human Relations Training.* (1972) (vols I – X).

Reddy, B. *Intervention Skills: Process Consultation for Small Groups and Teams.* (1994) Jossey-Bass/ Pfeiffer. San Francisco, CA.

Scholtes, P. R. *The Leader's Handbook.* (1998) McGraw-Hill. Toronto, Canada.

Schutz, W. C. *The Interpersonal Underworld.* (1966) Science and Behavior Books. Palo Alto, CA.

Tuckman, B. W. *Developmental Sequences in Small Groups.* (1965) Psychological Bulletin.

Wood, J. T., Phillips, G. M., and Pederson, D. J. *Group Discussion: A Practical Guide to Participation and Leadership.* 2nd ed. (1986) Harper and Row. New York, NY.

Zander, A. *Making Groups Effective.* (1983) Jossey-Bass. San Francisco, CA.

Chapter 4 – Consulting Strategies for Facilitators

Argyris, C. *Intervention Theory and Methods: A Behavioral Science View.* (1970) Addison-Wesley. Reading, MA.

Blake, R. R., and Mouton, J. S. *Consultation.* 2nd ed. (1983) Addison-Wesley. Reading, MA.

Block, P. *Flawless Consulting.* 2nd ed. (2000) Jossey-Bass/Pfeiffer. San Francisco, CA.

Bradford, L. P. *Making Meetings Work.* (1976) University Associates. San Diego, CA.

Brown, S., and Fisher, R. *Getting Together.* (1992) Penguin Publishing. New York, NY.

Cooper, S., and Heenan, C. *Preparing, Designing and Leading Workshops: A Humanistic Approach.* (1980) CBI Publishing Company. Boston, MA.

Dotlich, D., and Cairo, P. *Action Coaching.* (1999) Jossey-Bass. San Francisco, CA.

Dyer, W. G. *Team Building: Issues and Alternatives.* 2nd ed. (1987) Addison-Wesley. Reading, MA.

Fairhurst, G., and Sarr, R. *The Art of Framing.* (1996) Jossey-Bass, San Francisco, CA.

Harrison, R. "Choosing the Depth of Organizational Intervention." (1970) *The Journal of Applied Behavioral Science,* 1 (2), 181–202.

Heron, J. *Group Facilitation: Theories and Models for Practice.* (1993) Kogan Page, London, UK.

Howell, J. L. *Tools for Facilitating Team Meetings.* (1995) Integrity Publishing. Seattle, WA.

Lippitt, G., and Lippitt, R. *The Consulting Process in Action.* 2nd ed. (1986) Jossey-Bass. San Francisco, CA.

Payne, S. L. *The Art of Asking Questions.* (1951) Princeton University Press. Princeton, NJ.

Schein, E. H. *Process Consultation: Its Role in Organization Development.* (1969) Addison-Wesley. Reading, MA.

Schwarz, R. M. *The Skilled Facilitator.* (2002) Jossey-Bass. San Francisco, CA.

Strachen, D. *Questions that Work: A Resource for Facilitators.* (2001) ST Press. Ottawa, Canada.

Chapter 5 – Essential Processes for Facilitators

Albert, R., Dannemiller, K., Loup, R., and Jacobs, R. *Real Time Strategic Change: A Consultant's Guide to Large Scale Meetings.* (1994) Dannemiller Tyson Associates. Ann Arbor, MI.

Argyris, C., Putnam, R., and Smith, D. M. *Action Science.* (1985) Jossey-Bass. San Francisco, CA.

Beckhard, R., and Harris, R. *Organizational Transitions: Managing Complex Change.* 2nd ed. (1987) Addison-Wesley. Boston, MA.

Bunker, B., and Alban, B., "The Large Group Interaction—A New Social Innovation?" (1992) *Journal of Applied Behavioral Sciences.* 28(4), 473–479.

Dotlich, D., and Cairo, P. *Action Coaching.* (1999) Jossey-Bass. San Francisco, CA.

Eggleton, H. C., and Rice, J. C. *The Fieldbook of Team Interventions.* (1996) HRD Press. Amherst, MA.

Owen, H. *Open Space Technology: A User's Guide.* (1992) Abbott. Potomac, MD.

Senge, P. *The Fifth Discipline: The Art and Practice of the Learning Organization.* (1990) Doubleday. New York, NY.

Tague, N.R. *The Quality Toolbox.* (1995) ASQC Quality Press. Milwaukee, WI.

Weisbord, M. *Productive Workplaces: Organizing and Managing for Dignity, Meaning and Community.* (1980) Jossey-Bass. San Francisco, CA.

About the Author

INGRID BENS is a consultant and trainer whose special areas of expertise are facilitation skills, team building, conflict management, employee participation and organizational change.

Ingrid has a Master's Degree in Adult Education and more than 25 years' experience as a workshop leader and organization development consultant. Ingrid is the founder of Participative Dynamics, a consulting firm located in Sarasota, Florida, and a founding partner in Facilitation First located in Toronto, Canada.

Ingrid Bens is also the author of *Facilitating With Ease!* Jossey-Bass (2nd ed.), 2005.

Workshops Conducted by Participative Dynamics Include:

Core Facilitation Skills — 2 days

Hands-on, experiential techniques are used to get across the key concepts and allow for maximum practice and feedback. This workshop explores the role of the facilitator and teaches the fundamentals of how to manage group behavior, deal with group conflict, and use the main tools in the facilitator toolkit. Ideal for new project or team leaders, as well as team members.

Advanced Facilitation Skills — 2 days

Each advanced program is custom designed after an extensive needs assessment. Workshop content aims to help experienced facilitators gain breakthrough skills. Advanced curriculum topics include: overcoming resistance and gaining buy-in, managing group dynamics, making immediate interventions, advanced decision making, and creating facilitation designs.

Facilitating Win/Win — 3 days

A workshop designed to share facilitation tools and techniques with mediators. Begins with the two-day core facilitation skills workshop and then progresses through the five step Win-Win model using a negotiation case study. Participants are divided into parties and gain first-hand experience using essential tools and techniques in a dynamic team situation. Continuous practice and feedback support rapid skill development.

To read more about these workshops visit:
www.participative-dynamics.com

How to Use the Accompanying CD-ROM

System Requirements

PC with Microsoft Windows 98SE or later
Mac with Apple OS version 8.6 or later

Using the CD with Windows

To view the items located on the CD, follow these steps:

1. Insert the CD into your computer's CD-ROM drive.
2. A window appears with the following options:
   Contents: Allows you to view the files included on the CD-ROM.
   Software: Allows you to install useful software from the CD-ROM.
   Links: Displays a hyperlinked page of Web sites.
   Author: Displays a page with information about the Author(s).
   Help: Displays a page with information on using the CD.
   Exit: Closes the interface window.

If you do not have autorun enabled, or if the autorun window does not appear, follow these steps to access the CD:

1. Click Start -> Run.
2. In the dialog box that appears, type d:<\\>start.exe, where d is the letter of your CD-ROM drive. This brings up the autorun window described in the preceding set of steps.
3. Choose the desired option from the menu. (See Step 2 in the preceding list for a description of these options.)

Using the CD with a Mac

1. Insert the CD into your computer's CD-ROM drive.
2. The CD-ROM icon appears on your desktop; double-click the icon.
3. Double-click the Start icon.
4. A window appears with the following options:
   Contents: Allows you to view the files included on the CD-ROM.
   Software: Allows you to install useful software from the CD-ROM.

Links: Displays a hyperlinked page of Web sites.

Author: Displays a page with information about the Author(s).

Contact Us: Displays a page with information on contacting the publisher or author.

Help: Displays a page with information on using the CD.

Exit: Closes the interface window.

To Download Documents

The documents on this disk are in two application formats: Microsoft Word files and PDF files. To download a document, first open it. For Windows users, under the File pull-down menu, choose Save As, and save the document to your hard drive. You can also click on your CD drive in Windows Explorer and select a document to copy to your hard drive.

In Case of Trouble

If you experience difficulty using the CD-ROM, please follow these steps:

1. Make sure your hardware and systems configurations conform to the systems requirements noted under "System Requirements" above.
2. Review the installation procedure for your type of hardware and operating system. It is possible to reinstall the software if necessary.

To speak with someone in Product Technical Support, call 800-762-2974 or 317-572-3994 M–F 8:30a.m.–5:00p.m. EST. You can also get support and contact Product Technical Support at http://www.wiley.com/techsupport.

Before calling or writing, please have the following information available:

- Type of computer and operating system
- Any error messages displayed
- Complete description of the problem

It is best if you are sitting at your computer when making the call.